ONE WAY

Do you have to believe in Christ to be saved?

Hywel R. Jones

Published in association with FIEC by

DayOnepublications

Most scripture quotations are from The New International Version © 1973, 1978, 1984, International Bible Society. Published by Hodder and Stoughton.

ISBN 0 902548 70 0

Published by Day One Publications
6 Sherman Road, Bromley, Kent BR1 3JH

Designed by Steve Devane and printed by Clifford Frost Ltd, Wimbledon SW19 2SE

Dedication
This book is dedicated to the members of the Westminster
Fellowship of Ministers

Acknowledgements

As I complete this book I am aware that an expression of thanks is due to many people who have given encouragement and advice with regard to its subject matter and method of treatment. I hope this word of appreciation will be accepted by all those to whom I am indebted and that they will be pleased with the result of our co-operation.

Some, however, must be identified. There are, first, the members of the Theological Committee of the Fellowship of Independent Evangelical Churches who supplied the initial stimulus to consider this theme. I am grateful to them and in particular to the Rev. Andrew Anderson for so many improvements to the text which he suggested. Secondly, my colleagues at the London Theological Seminary have, as usual, assisted me. Finally, the members of the Westminster Fellowship of Ministers provided particular help when some of its subject matter was discussed at one of their regular meetings. It is to them that this book is dedicated with the prayer that the position which it presents will be their continued belief and the theme of their preaching.

London Theological Seminary

January 1996

ONE WAY

FACING THE ISSUE is a series of books designed to help Christians to think biblically on a variety of pressing issues that confront evangelicals at the present time. The themes are primarily theological but, as the Bible never teaches doctrine in isolation, all have a keen practical edge to them.

The series began its life in the cut and thrust of discussion in the Theological Committee of the Fellowship of Independent Evangelical Churches whose brief is to monitor and respond to challenges and changes in the world of evangelical theology. The committee, whose members currently are Brian Edwards (chair), Andrew Anderson, Paul Brown, Andrew Bryant, David Field, Stanley Jebb, Hywel Jones and Jonathan Stephen, commissions the writers, discusses their approach with them, and is available for consultation. Though united in our understanding of the gospel, we do not always come to exactly the same conclusions on every detail. So the views put forward by the authors do not necessarily reflect in every respect those of the committee or, for that matter, those of the FIEC or the Publisher.

The series is written with the general reader in mind and the books do not assume a background training in theology. They are, however, written by men of proven ability in grappling with important theological trends. We hope that each book will stimulate thought and action, both controlled by the Bible.

Andrew Anderson
Series Editor

Yet here a question may be asked, Whether faith require the knowledge of Christ, or it be content with the simple persuasion of the mercy of God? for Cornelius seemeth to have known nothing at all concerning Christ. But it may be proved by sound proofs that faith cannot be separated from Christ; for if we lay hold upon the bare majesty of God, we are rather confounded by his glory, than that we feel any taste of his goodness. Therefore, Christ must come between, that the mind of man may conceive that God is merciful. And it is not without cause that he is called the image of the invisible God, (Col.1.15;) because the Father offereth himself to be holden in his face alone. Moreover, seeing that he is the way, the truth, and the life, (John 14.6;) whithersoever thou goest without him, thou shalt be enwrapped on every side in errors, and death shall meet you on every side'.[1]

(John Calvin commenting on Acts 10: 4)

' I have now to ask whether you can consent to part from your daughter early next spring, to see her no more in this world; whether you can consent to her departure, and her subjection to the hardships and sufferings of a missionary life; whether you can consent to her exposure to the dangers of the ocean; to the fatal influence of the southern climate of India; to every kind of want and distress; to degradation, insult, persecution and perhaps a violent death. Can you consent to all this, for the sake of him who left his heavenly home, and died for her and for you; for the sake of perishing immortal souls; for the sake of Zion and the glory of God? Can you consent to all this, in hope of soon meeting your daughter in the world of glory, with the crown of righteousness, brightened with the acclamations of praise which shall redound to her Saviour from heathens saved, through her means, from eternal woe and despair?'[2]

(Adoniram Judson, missionary to Burma, in a letter written in 1810 to John Hasseltine asking for his daughter's hand in marriage)

ENDNOTES

1. Commentary on the Acts of the Apostles. John Calvin Vol 1 Eerdmans 1957 p. 413
2. To the Golden Shore The Life of Adoniram Judson. Courtney Anderson Judson Press 1987 p.83

Charting our course

'What must I do to be saved?' is the most important single question any one could ever ask. Its significance can be gauged from the fact that it is recorded in Holy Scripture not merely once, in those familiar words, but more than once though in other terms. Here is a question everyone ought to ask; the answer is something that everyone ought to know.

In the Old Testament, Job asked 'How can a mortal be righteous before God?' (Job 9:2). In the New Testament, a Jewish lawyer asked 'What good thing must I do to get eternal life?' (Matthew 19:16) and several Jews asked 'What shall we do that we may work the works of God?' (John 6:28) These are all variations on the single theme voiced by the non-Jewish jailor at Philippi 'What must I do to be saved?' (Acts 16:30)

But the Bible does more than merely record the question. It also provides an answer to it - an answer which is one and the same in substance although it is expressed in different words according to time and place. 'Believe in the Lord Jesus Christ and you will be saved' (Acts 16:31) is a summary of it. Paul said that to a Gentile. To the Jews, Jesus said 'This is the work of God that you believe on him who He has sent'. (John 6.29)

THE MAINSTREAM POSITION

Believing in the Lord Jesus Christ is therefore the way to heaven which the Bible teaches, and that applies to everyone. This book affirms that position which can justly be called the mainstream view of the Christian church. It is true that statements advocating a different position, or recognising such a possibility, have been made by theologians but these have been occasional and isolated. Up to the present time, no consistent body of alternative opinion has developed, survived and won the day. The confessional statements which approach this matter are the seventeenth century Westminster Confession of Faith, The Savoy Declaration and the 1689 Baptist Confession. As we shall see, they do not teach the salvation of the heathen. But the situation is changing.

This mainstream position has come to be denominated by the technical term 'Exclusivism'. While that word is not wholly inaccurate because something exclusive is being affirmed, it is unfortunate in that it carries some pejorative associations. It is therefore worth stressing two things. First, this exclusivism has not only been compatible with great missionary activity; it lies close to the mainspring of it. Secondly, the church has not become exclusive on this matter in the twentieth century; it always has been so. 'Exclusivism' is no recent development in the church. Harold Netland, a contemporary missionary teacher and author, has written:

> 'Historically, exclusivism has been the dominant position of the Christian church'.[1]

Then, John E. Sanders, who does not himself adopt this position, has also acknowledged the self same fact. He has written:

> 'This position has been widespread throughout the history of the church and appears to be the dominant view in contemporary evangelical thought'.[2]

In addition, Netland reminds us that

> 'Christian exclusivism is by no means an oddity when considered in the broader context of the global religious traditions'.[3]

OTHER VIEWS

This book upholds what may therefore be quite fairly called the traditional or classical position and aims to restate it by way of interaction with different views which are being currently expressed on this subject.

In the churches at large, many now question the exclusive saviourhood of Jesus Christ. To deny that the Lord Jesus Christ is the only saviour of sinners is devastating. It not only deprives the church of a unique message to the world but also undermines and corrupts her own distinctiveness.

But even within the evangelical constituency, there are those who are currently proposing other answers to the all important question which we mentioned at the very beginning. While affirming that Christ is the only Saviour, they deny the necessity of explicit faith in him so they do not say that the only way of salvation is by believing on the Lord Jesus Christ. The main negative purpose of this book is to present what they are saying and to respond to it by evaluating what they teach in the light of Scripture.

Two evangelicals who have written most strongly on this subject, advocating a different line from the mainstream view, are Peter Cotterell and Clark Pinnock. The former is the recent Principal of the London Bible College and his views on this subject are recorded in his book entitled 'Mission and Meaninglessness'.[4] The latter, a Canadian, did postgraduate study in Manchester and is now lecturing at McMaster Divinity College in Ontario. He has written fully on this subject in a book entitled 'A Wideness in God's Mercy'.[5]

While Cotterell and Pinnock do not expound an identical position in detail, they do agree in declaring that it is *not* essential for everyone to believe in Jesus Christ in order to go to heaven. Indeed, they actually teach that some, perhaps many, who *cannot* so believe because they have never heard the gospel, *will* be there. We want to examine the grounds on which they base that claim because they deny that they are teaching salvation by works and not grace, and maintain that they are asserting salvation in Christ alone. What they are denying is that faith in Christ is a sine qua non of salvation.

But there are others who have written on this subject and their number is growing. W.Gary Phillips asserts that what used to be an 'overwhelming evangelical consensus' in favour of Exclusivism has been broken up. Referring to the associated beliefs of the unevangelised being lost unless they believe the gospel and the endlessness of their punishment, he writes:

> 'A recent survey of evangelical college and seminary students showed that 32 percent and 31 percent (respectively) no longer hold these teachings'.[6]

The evidence for this survey is found in a book published in Chicago by J.D.Hunter entitled 'Evangelicalism: The Coming Generation'. Hunter is quoted by Phillips as follows:

> 'The existence of such a sizable minority of Evangelicals maintaining this (new) stance represents a noteworthy shift away from the historical interpretations ... If historical precedent is instructive, it becomes clear that these tendencies will probably escalate'.[7]

Given all this, it is not surprising that the subject was discussed at plenary and other sessions of the 1989 Annual Meeting of the Evangelical Theological Society. The journal of that society had carried an article one month before that meeting entitled 'Those Who Have Never Heard: Have They No Hope?'[8] In 1991 a symposium appeared to which nineteen seminary professors contributed.[9] Reviewing this volume, Ramesh Richard makes the significant comment:

> 'The book shows a dire need for multiple contributions from those who have been dealing with this exact issue for centuries. Here I refer to scholars in parts of the world where evangelical Christianity as a minority religion has constantly had to face the majority culture/religion with firm answers'.[10]

There is an implied rebuke in that comment of a western world which has gone soft or lost its nerve.

This matter is of such theological and practical importance that it requires an examination and a response. It is inevitable that the alternative view to the one which is being advocated in this book will have an adverse effect on the making known of the way of life across the globe. But even more than that is at stake. Richard writes:

> 'The very denotation of the word "evangelical" hinges around a biblically faithful, logically consistent and sociologically relevant reading of the topic of religious pluralism'.[11]

In undertaking our task we therefore hope that this book will serve the positive purpose of encouraging Christian preachers and witnesses in this and other countries to make known the only way to life to any and to all.

METHOD OF APPROACH

The method which will be followed in this book is ably and memorably summarised by John Wesley, the evangelist and missionary who laid claim to 'the world' as his parish. He wrote the following words:

> 'I have thought, I am a creature of a day, passing through life as an arrow through the air. I am a spirit come from God, and returning to God: just hovering over the great gulf; till a few moments hence , I am no more seen; I drop into an unchangeable eternity! I want to know one thing, the way to heaven ... God himself has condescended to teach the way; for this very thing he came from heaven. He hath written it down in a book. O give me that book: At any price give me the book of God! I have it: here is knowledge enough for me. Let me be homo unius libri (i.e. the man of one book). Here then I am far from the busy ways of men. I sit down alone: only God is here. In his presence I open, I read His book; for this end, to find the way to heaven ... Is there a doubt concerning the meaning of what I read? Does anything appear dark and intricate? I lift up my heart to the Father of lights:- "Lord, is it not

thy word 'If any man lack wisdom, let him ask of
God?'" Thou 'givest liberally and upbraidest not' Thou
hast said 'If any be willing to do thy will, he shall
know' I am willing to do, let me know, thy will. I then
search after and consult parallel passages of Scripture,
"comparing spiritual things with spiritual". I meditate
thereon with all the attention and earnestness of which
my mind is capable. If any doubt still remain, I consult
those who are experienced in the things of God: and
then the writings whereby, being dead, they yet speak.
And what I thus learn, that I teach'.[12]

From these words of a man whose evangelistic zeal cannot be doubted we can learn how we ought to approach this subject as all others. His statement is a summary of a truly evangelical doctrine of Scripture and its interpretation. It is a reminder to us that it is only as Scripture is approached *properly*, that is with a mind and spirit which is in accord with its character as well as an examination of the text in its smaller and larger context, that the end result will correspond to God's truth on what is being studied.

The principles which inform Wesley's approach are as follows:

1. Scripture is God's book in the sense that is written by him and he teaches by it. Its teaching should therefore be determinative for us on all that it presents.

2. God has set out the way to heaven in Scripture; otherwise it could not be known by anyone. To conceive that there is another way beside or beyond what is recorded is to impugn the nature of God as well as to arrogate to oneself a status which cannot belong to a sinful mortal.

3. There are two helps to understand Scripture's teaching which are open to all who accept it as God's book. The first is prayer to God for enlightenment as one reads and the second is considering other passages in Scripture which are relevant to the matter under examination. Both are to be done in the realisation that one is in the presence of God.

4. If some uncertainty remains, because not everything in Scripture is immediately plain and obvious to all, recourse is to be made to those who have been taught by God, both those who are alive in the present and those from the past who still speak by their writings.

5. What is learned of God's truth is to be proclaimed to the world of mankind.

We list these principles at the outset for two reasons. First, they are the guidelines which we will seek to follow in the treatment of this book. Secondly, there is evidence that evangelicals are not following these principles as firmly as they ought. We would therefore encourage the reader to follow Wesley's advice and study the Bible prayerfully to see if the things which are presented in this book are true (Acts 17:11b). The fact that on one occasion Wesley himself seemed to waver on this matter is an example of human inconsistency. He not only refused to lay blame on those who never heard the gospel for failing to believe it but regarded it as possible that some heathen might have been taught the essentials of true religion.[13]

Our procedure will be first to examine Acts 4:12. This text is arguably the strongest expression of Christian exclusivism which is found in the New Testament. Doing this will provide us with the opportunity to respond in general terms to the views current in the wider church scene which have been referred to earlier. It will also indicate what some evangelicals are saying about the particular subject area to be examined in these pages.

Secondly, consideration will be given to the arguments which Cotterell presents in favour of the position that all outside of Christ cannot be justly condemned. Then we will look at Pinnock's treatment of what Scripture says about certain non-Israelites (Jews) and non-Christians being saved. These chapters are the storm centre of this book.

Having set aside both those positions, we will look at some alternative views which are to be located somewhere between exclusivism and the optimism which they, and others, represent. Finally, we will set out some statements from the Epistle to the Romans which seem to speak definitively on the main aspects of this subject.

ENDNOTES

1. Dissonant Voices. Religious Pluralism and the Question of Truth H.A.Netland Apollos 1991 p.10

2. Is Belief in Christ Necessary For Salvation? J.E.Sanders Evangelical Quarterly Vol 60 No.3 1988 pp.242,3

3. Netland op.cit.p.35

4. Mission and Meaninglessness. The good news in a world of suffering and disorder. Peter Cotterell SPCK 1990

5. A Wideness in God's Mercy. The Finality of Jesus Christ in a World of Religions. Clark H. Pinnock Zondervan 1992

6. Evangelicals and Pluralism: Current Options. W.Gary Phillips Evangelical Quarterly Vol 64 No 3 1992 pp.229,30

7. ibid.pp.229,30

8. E.D.Osburn Journal of the Evangelical Theological Society Vol 32 No.3 1989

9. Through No Fault Of Their Own: The Fate of those Who Have Never Heard. eds.W.V.Crockett & J.G.Sigountos. Baker 1991

10. Evangelical Review of Theology Vol 18 No.1 1994 p.80

11. ibid.p.70

12. Forty Four Sermons Epworth Press 1952 p.vi

13. Wesley's Works Vol vi p.286; Vol vii pp.196-9,258,353.

No other name?

Two books published recently bear the same title, 'No Other Name'. Both are written by North American scholars. One is by Paul Knitter, a Roman Catholic, and the other by John Sanders, an evangelical. Neither endorses the exclusivist (mainstream) understanding of the statement in Acts 4:12. 'There is no salvation in any other ...' Even so, they do not treat that statement in the same way, as we shall see.

The title of Knitter's book[1] is followed by a question mark, the significance of which is explained in the book's sub-title 'A Critical Survey of Christian Attitudes Towards the World Religions'. Knitter is setting aside what we may call the plain meaning of Acts 4:12 and he does so on a twofold basis. First, he is a universalist including the followers of other religions within the scope of salvation. Secondly, he regards the language which Peter used in Acts 4:12 as being devotional not doctrinal, only expressing love to Jesus Christ and consecration to his service but saying nothing about the condition or destiny of non-Christians.

Knitter is not alone in adopting this outlook. The Protestant theologian John Hick, with whom Knitter has co-operated[2] and his teacher the late Karl Rahner,[3] a Jesuit theologian, have also advocated it, notwithstanding differences between them. The titles of several books which have been published in the last twenty years or so, for example John Hick's 'God and the Universe of Faiths' and 'God has Many Names' and Raymond Pannikar's 'The Unknown Christ of Hinduism', indicate that there is a large field to investigate on this matter.

The Second Vatican Council of the Roman Catholic Church gave a great boost to the recognition of other religions as expressions of a genuine seeking after God on the part of many. This is found in the

'Declaration on the Relationship of the Church to Non-Christian Religions' referred to as 'Nostra Aetate', its opening words in Latin, and also in 'The Dogmatic Constitution on the Church', called 'Lumen Gentium'. This was the first time that the Roman Catholic Church faced this issue head on and spoke definitively on the matter.

In doing so, it contradicted its famous dictum 'extra ecclesiam nulla salus est' (outside the Church there is no salvation) which had governed its attitude to all non-Catholics. It also went beyond the notion of 'baptism of desire' by which the true and the good in other religions were regarded as belonging to the church albeit unknowingly, to include some recognition of the partial but none the less real value of their religions. Carl Henry has written:

> *'John Paul II reportedly holds that the universal search for faith already embraces an implicitly genuine faith and this satisfies the necessary condition for salvation'.*[4]

The following statements of the Second Vatican Council have had an influence well beyond the boundaries of the Roman Church:

> *'The Catholic Church rejects nothing of what is true and holy in these religions. She has a high regard for the manner of life and conduct, the precepts and doctrines which, although differing in many ways from her own teaching, nevertheless often reflect a ray of that truth which enlightens all men'.*[5]

Further with regard to people themselves and in particular those who have never heard, it declares:

> *'Those who, through no fault of their own, do not know the Gospel of Christ or his Church, but who nevertheless seek God with a sincere heart, and, moved by grace, try in their actions to do his will as they know it through the dictates of their conscience-those too may be saved'.*[6]

But let us move to the evangelical side. The title of Sanders' book[7] does not have a question mark. It does, however, have an exclamation mark and a significant sub-title which indicates the precise point which is agitating contemporary evangelicalism. It reads 'A Biblical, Historical and Theological Investigation into the Destiny of the Unevangelized'. Sanders declares that he fully accepts the positive and explicit assertion in Acts 4:12 that salvation is only to be found in the Lord Jesus Christ, but not the corollary that all who are unevangelised will be condemned. It is that corollary - the destiny of the unevangelized - which is the precise focus of this book. We will postpone an examination of Sanders' exposition until we have completed our own study of Acts 4:12.

ACTS 4:12

This is a most important verse of Scripture at this time not only in relation to the church's task in the world but also with regard to her thinking about the gospel. As it is a statement of the gospel which is found in the Bible, it provides us with an example of how close the linkage is between them. The gospel is found in the Bible, infallibly presented there in all sorts of ways. The Bible, therefore, supports the gospel which, in turn, leads those who receive it to the Bible. The one serves the interests of the other. There is, however, another side to this connection - a dark one. It is that, when either the Bible or the gospel is undermined, the other is bound to be adversely affected. One cannot play down the Bible and play up the gospel.

In the early part of this century, attempts were made to speak well of Jesus and of the gospel while challenging the infallibility of the Bible. The threat which is currently posed to the gospel is therefore the direct result of that threat which was posed to the Bible in the early decades of this century, and even before that. As an inevitable consequence of the departure from an orthodox doctrine of Scripture, we now find in the wider church that the gospel is at stake. If the church cannot say 'No other book' in relation to a divinely inspired account of saving revelation, it will soon be unable to say 'No other Name' in relation to the exclusiveness of Jesus Christ as Saviour. While some Christians did not see that Christianity itself was threatened in the conflict over Scripture, it is to be hoped that they may see that now in the conflict over the gospel!

The book of the Acts of the Apostles records how Christianity spread from Jerusalem to Rome, from a group of 120 Jews to include thousands of Jews and non-Jews, from something in an upstairs room to something which turned the world upside down. Acts 4:12 relates to a particular occasion when the gospel was made known and people were affected. The transformation took place primarily through the proclamation of the good news of Jesus Christ, the only Saviour. So in Acts 4:12 we find instruction in the task of spreading the gospel in our multi-racial, multi-religious and pagan world and hopefully, the inspiration to do so. Acts 4:12 is what the church of today ought to be saying and how it ought to be saying it. But, by and large, she is no longer able to do either. This is most serious because Acts 4:12 is an utterance of the apostles, Peter and John, who were sent personally by Jesus Christ, authorised to make known his truth. Acts 4:12 is therefore of considerable significance for the church in every time and culture. It supplies a standard to which all Christian proclamation should conform. Unless it is acceptable to the church, her proclamation of the Christian message will neither be in truth nor in power.

An example of the way in which one's view of the Bible as the word of God is linked closely with one's view of Acts 4:12 is found in the words of David L. Edwards. In his book examining the evangelical convictions of John Stott, to which Stott responded, he wrote on Acts 4:12 as follows:

> 'This one text, which arises out of a story of a crippled beggar, is sometimes thought to settle the eternal destiny of all but a fraction of mankind. I am one of those who believe (with the Second Vatican Council) that it does no such thing. It seems ludicrous to suggest that the problem of the non-Christians is settled by these few words, found in an account of a speech said to have been delivered by Peter to the Sanhedrin in Jerusalem with only one other Christian (John) present about half a century before the Acts of the Apostles was written. For the problem is about centuries and continents about which Luke and Peter knew nothing or next to nothing'.[8]

It is also instructive to see how Acts 4:12 has been treated in commentaries written in the last hundred years. What emerges from such a review is a confirmation that something deleterious has happened in the churches over that period. We will just sketch that picture, noting as we proceed to do so that there are no textual variations in the extant manuscripts of the verse.

Taking 1878 as a rough departure point, we find in the commentaries of J. A. Alexander[9] and H. A. W. Meyer[10] that Acts 4:12 presented them with no exegetical problems at all. They commented on all its terms and stated its obvious meaning. But a change becomes noticeable in the first decades of this century. The verse was only commented on in general terms by Furneaux[11] ; Foakes-Jackson[12], Rackham[13] and others[14]. This relative silence is ominous. It is hardly a case of letting parts of the text speak for themselves. In the years following the Second World War, the obvious meaning of the verse is either argued with or explained away.[15]

But sadly, it is not only liberal commentators who fail to do justice to the verse. As long ago as 1951, F.F.Bruce possibly opened a door to a weakened interpretation of this verse when he wrote :

'The emphasis is on the one name that is given rather than on any other in which there is no salvation'.[16]

Two other weaknesses in evangelical commentaries on this verse call for comment, namely those by Howard Marshall[17] and John Stott.[18] In the first, the words 'under heaven' are not emphasised and in the second the expression 'none other' is not highlighted. The words 'under heaven' indicate a scope of reference which goes beyond the meaning of 'among men'. They stress universality and not just presence among mankind. The words 'none other' express strongly the element of rejection of every other name. Those dimensions of meaning in the text are not brought out as clearly as they ought to be and as clearly as Kistemaker does in his commentary.[19]

Clearly Acts 4:12 is a good litmus test of the church's condition, its relative health and vigour, or its decline and weakness. We shall try to show that evangelicals need to test themselves by it, or allow it to test them, as well as insisting on testing others by it. It is a sign of the times that Acts 4:12 which was originally intended to exert pressure on the unbelieving, seems today to put pressure on the church. Nearly everything in it is objectionable to so much of the contemporary church. Indeed, it is almost as if the Lord God moved Peter to say it with the late twentieth century in view rather than the first! Of course he did not do that: but what he did was to move him to utter it in the first century with the twentieth century also in view.

Acts 4:12 censures and vetoes many of the most cherished notions of churches today and at the same time recalls the church to his truth and encourages her to proclaim it. We will consider this statement under three headings.

THE FORM OF ACTS 4:12

We begin by looking at the literary form of this verse. Even on that relatively superficial level, it has something important to say by way of a critique of so much in contemporary Christianity. Acts 4:12 is in statement form. It is not a question. Peter is not asking for information; he is conveying it. He is making an assertion and not inviting comment. This is proclamation not dialogue.

But something more needs to be said about its form. Though Acts 4:12 is an assertion, it is cast in the negative. There are not only negative terms in the verse; the whole verse is a negation. Even the clause at the end, 'whereby we must be saved', carries a strong negative inference because it indicates that being saved is no optional matter. There can be no reasonable doubt that Peter, the apostle, was intending to deny certain things when he said what he did. No one listening to him would have thought otherwise.

Negations are not that plentiful in contemporary theology, academic or popular, or in eccclesiastical pronouncements about mission - unless it be in response to someone who makes negations! The only thing which seems to be clearly denied in today's church is that denials can be properly and graciously expressed; that is that any one can speak as Peter did. All kinds of evasions are practised to avoid having to say that something is wrong or untrue. This is not just a case of being respectful or wise. It is evidence that there is a presupposition, even a prejudice at work, one which regards denials and exclusions as being at least ill-informed or, at worst, bigoted, and obscurantist.

What then is to be made of Peter's negation? Was he carried away by the heat of the moment, speaking with vehemence but not much thought - something which he had been prone to do? In a rather superior manner, it has been assumed that he would have wished, on reflection, to tone down his statement. Such psychologising by non-professionals is hazardous enough when the patient is on the couch. But when it is attempted at a distance of 2,000 years, it takes some doing - and some believing!

When one looks at the verse in its context, a very different picture emerges. Peter was *moved* - who wouldn't be? But he was thinking as well as feeling, and feeling what he was thinking. Indeed, his thinking was clear and elevated because he was 'filled with the Spirit'. This can best be seen by examining his declaration closely. We look first at the connection between the two parts of verse 12 and then at the relationship between verse 12a and verse 11.

Verse 12

The two parts of this verse are linked by the preposition 'for' which means 'because'. So the negation which comes first is substantiated by the explanation which follows. Clearly Peter was thinking; he was reasoning and not exploding in mindless passion. He was making a considered statement, namely that there was salvation in no one else *because* (for) no one else has been given by heaven (God) to human beings as a Saviour.

Verse 12 &11a

But that is not all. The negation is itself deduced from the statement which precedes it and that statement (verse 11) is a quotation from Psalm 118. In other words it is from the Old Testament and so is a word from God himself. The negation is therefore in the nature of a conclusion drawn from divine revelation. Peter was thinking biblically. For him, there were firm statements made in Scripture from which equally firm conclusions could be drawn 'theo-logically'. The one yielded the other. God's affirmations yield negations of their logical opposites. Every thesis has an antithesis. That is an element in apostolic theology as well as in logic.

Few theologians today follow the theological method of the apostle. That is the root problem, and as a consequence the church is adrift. It has cut itself loose from the anchor of revealed inscripturated truth and the chain of logical theological method.

The account of Paul's voyage to Rome in Acts 27 and the storm which engulfed the ship on which he was travelling, the jettisoning of the cargo and the real risk of ruin, present an accurate picture of the church in these days. This is made strikingly clear by the titles of two books of essays published in the sixties, which are actually derived from this chapter. They are' Up and down in Adria' and 'Soundings' (cf. Acts 27:27&28) and they describe a drifting church and an attempt to find an anchorage.

Theology is now governed by an existentialist outlook which means that truth is what has become true for each and every individual - the liberal and the radical; the ecumenical as well as the evangelical; the Roman Catholic as well as the Protestant; the Muslim, the Jew, the Hindu as well as the Christian. There is nothing which is absolutely authoritative for all. 'It all depends what you mean …' and 'This is how it appears to me' are the order of the day. God's self-disclosure in Scripture does not include definitive statements but only explanations of divine-human encounters. To use the jargon, revelation is only personalist and not propositional as well.

As a result, the study of theology has become essentially pluralist in character and method. There is not one book and one religion in the light of which one can or should view all others. All are to be taken into account in much the same terms. Pluralism is setting everything on the same plane and looking at everything together. John Hick has declared 'Truth is two eyed'. By that he means that a statement and what seems to be its logical opposite are both aspects of truth. Archbishop Runcie has said that truth has a thousand eyes! This means that somehow everything is part of truth.

If one cannot make and live with Peter's negation, one is not only disagreeing with apostolic Christianity but also with the nature of truth. Truth is one and consistent; incarnate in Christ and inscripturated in the Bible. While it is rich and many-sided, it is harmonious. Contradictions of it are wrong; they are unreal and soul-destroying notions. Truth has an opposite: everything is not true. Its antithesis is error. Thinking of that kind is basic to true science; its opposite is in the nature of non-sense. Divine revelation is not contrary to reason. The truth of the matter is that it is so far above reason that it appears to be contrary to reason to all who do not have true faith.

In the summer of 1989, the Independent newspaper carried comments from a number of invited contributors on the subject of how the major world religions relate to each other. Paul Helm, then of Liverpool University, but now Professor at King's College, London, was among those invited to contribute. He pointed out that, in all the pieces which had been published prior to his, there was a 'notable absentee'. This he identified as 'any concern for truth'. He wrote:

> 'Pilate's question "What is truth?" when it was originally asked, was no doubt the question of a cynic who would not wait for an answer. But modern enquiries into the relations between the faiths are in a different case. They do not even ask the question'.

He then went on to point out that, while a serious and fervent pursuit of truth characterised the disciplines of the natural sciences and the humanities, this was not the case among theologians. And the reason for that is simple. It lies in the nature of contemporary theological method which is linked to an unbiblical theology of revelation and reasoning.

We must not hesitate about making negations. Pressure is building up among evangelicals to avoid doing so. 'Be positive' is the cry. Of course, we are not to become negativistic and hyper-critical. But if we are not prepared to negate as clearly and loudly as we affirm then we are less than biblical and our affirmations will be left open to (re-) interpretation by the world and some in the church. Negations have a twofold positive function. They differentiate truth from error and determine the point at which an alleged interpretation of the former becomes in reality the latter. But they also declare the truth positively and clearly and that was what Peter wanted to do.

THE FOCUS OF ACTS 4:12

The statement which we are considering focuses on the matter of salvation. Whatever is said in this verse is related in some way or other to salvation which is its obvious focal point. It is referred to at the beginning by means of a noun (salvation) and then at the end by the use of a verb (be saved). As the verb is in the passive mood it is clear that human beings cannot save themselves. They need salvation to be provided for them - and God does so. But what is this 'salvation'?

In the early decades of this century, when the old 'social gospel' reigned, the use of the term 'salvation' was inevitably associated with 'fundamentalists'. It was their stock in trade, so to speak. It expressed their common belief in the universal reality of sin, in guilt, death, hell and Satan's power and in acceptance with God through the atonement accomplished by Christ, which brought forgiveness and eternal life to all who repented and believed. It was the evangelicals' language. No longer is that the case: others use the term and do so with a variety of meanings. We shall consider two which are being used by those who comment on this verse.

Salvation = Healing

First of all, several commentaries point out that Acts 4:12 is set in a healing context and the word 'saved' is a translation of the same Greek word as the word 'healed'. In addition, the word plainly means 'well' or 'in good health' at the end of verse 10. Why then, it is asked, may not the word 'healed' be substituted for the word 'saved' in verse 12? After all, Peter and John are responding to the question of the Sanhedrin concerning the healing which had taken place the day before.

Peter's answer to the question 'By what power or what name did you do this?' (v 7) runs from verse 8 to verse 12, the verse being examined. It is therefore claimed that in the answer which he gives he is only talking about physical healing and, by extension, psychological well being. Such thinking is reflected in the reports which the Inter-Faith Consultative Group of the Board for Mission and Unity of the Church of England produced in 1981 and also the Board for World Mission and Unity of the Church of Scotland in 1993. Acts 4:12 is regarded as being part of a story about healing and the authority by which that took place.

Salvation = Liberation from Injustice

Secondly, the term 'salvation' is understood by some as referring to liberty from every kind of oppression. This is the outlook of Liberation Theology which has come to the fore since the late sixties. Considered in this way, salvation amounts to freedom from every kind of socio-economic tyranny with all the deprivation which such oppression and concentration of wealth and power inevitably creates. The Third Assembly of the Commission on World Mission and Evangelism, a department of the World Council of Churches, held in Bangkok in 1973 was immediately preceded by a world conference called to discuss the subject of 'Salvation Today'. In this conference, salvation was regarded as having four dimensions, economic, social, political and personal. Due to the heavy influence of liberation theologies and anti-western third world theologies, all of the time was taken up in discussing the first three.

But what did Peter mean by the term 'salvation' when he answered the question put to him by the Sanhedrin? That is the all important inquiry. There is no doubt that the 'salvation word group' can include every aspect of restoration to wholeness and well-being within its range of meaning and there can therefore be no strong objection to including liberation from unjust rule or physical healing within its scope. But *the noun* 'salvation' is never used in that very general way in the entire New Testament. In addition, it ought to be noted that when Peter wished to refer to the miraculous physical healing which had taken place he used another noun, translated 'complete healing' (see Acts 3:16). These two facts suggest that 'salvation' in Acts 4:12 has some other meaning.

A second consideration is that Peter's answer concerning how the man had been healed is given by his mentioning the name of Jesus Christ of Nazareth. The physical healing is explained by the end of verse 10 and Peter then seizes the opportunity to preach Christ. Verses 11 and 12 are therefore in the nature of an exposition of the significance of 'The Name' and that cannot just refer either to healing, or to liberation from injustice which is alien to the context. Peter is talking about something other than either the healing of the body or the gaining of civil rights, both of which will be temporary in a fallen world. What does he have in mind by 'salvation?'

He illustrates it in terms of a cornerstone or capstone (v.11): the 'salvation' which he has in mind (v. 12) is depicted by the function of such a stone in the construction of an edifice. The words he quotes (v. 11) are taken from Psalm 118, a messianic Psalm. Jesus quotes it with reference to himself. (Matthew 21:42) It was one of the Psalms sung at Passover time. The building referred to by implication in the statements is a temple - a place where God dwells with his people.

A cornerstone is the first stone to be laid in the construction of a building; a copestone, the last. The cornerstone determines the whole lay-out of the building by setting the lines of the walls and their respective angles to each other. The copestone completes the edifice. The divine messiah therefore brings the 'new' temple into being and brings it to its completion. This stone is divinely chosen and placed. It is 'given'. 'No-one can lay any foundation other than the one already laid' (1 Corinthians 3:11).

J. A. Alexander wrote as follows concerning the term translated 'salvation' and his words are well worth heeding. He says that it is:

> 'the standing, not to say, the technical expression for the whole remedial work which the Messiah was to accomplish, and of which his personal name (Jesus) was significant'.[20]

That is why the definite article is used in the text: 'the' salvation. As such it is not to be identified with the renovation of the individual spirit alone. This would be to narrow it down to unjustifiable limits. It stands for the restoration of all things; a new world, i.e. new heavens and a new earth. It must therefore include the ultimate healing of the physical body which is its resurrection in glory and power and a realm where sin cannot enter.

But while this is so, the Scriptures teach that this 'salvation' is worked out or bestowed in stages through time, culminating only in eternity. The Bible teaches that while salvation will make people completely whole, it will not do so all at once or all on earth. The consummation will be at Christ's return.

To make salvation include physical healing and psychological wholeness for all and universal social justice in the *here and now* is therefore a serious and unbiblical distortion. Healings may and do occur; social harmony and justice may be found, primarily and increasingly in the church and, in striking measure, in the world during times of revival, but fully only in heaven. It is only when sin is forever banished and people are forever glorified that 'there will be no more pain ... and all the former things will have passed away'.

Even so, that entire 'salvation' which is secured by Christ comes by way of a complete package. It is associated with the bestowal of its initial blessings; namely repentance and the remission of sins (Acts 5:31). Those blessings can therefore be termed 'salvation' and what conveys them, 'the Gospel'. Acts 4:12 therefore, holds out the promise of salvation, smaller and larger; begun, continued, but consummated in heaven and not on earth and asserts that it is only found in Jesus Christ. It is divine, immense: it is 'so great' (Hebrews 2:3).

The Features of Acts 4:12

Peter uses other important expressions in this verse which bear upon its central term 'salvation' and these declare its exclusiveness and universality. Each of these needs to be emphasised today, separately and together.

a) Exclusiveness

Acts 4:12 makes it clear not only that this salvation is found in Jesus Christ but that it is found in him *alone*. There is no other saviour beside him and no salvation except in him. This amounts to a declaration of exclusiveness in the matter of salvation, a note which is not generally acceptable today. Such thinking is regarded as the mark of the rabid and bigoted fundamentalist, whatever may be his or her religion.

To avoid this opprobrium, many have preferred to use the term 'unique' instead of 'exclusive'. By that substitution an attempt is made to do justice to Jesus as one of his own kind without implying that there is no other like him. But it is not possible to define the word 'unique' without including the meaning and the force of the word 'exclusive'. To try to do so is to play a word game which only succeeds in exposing the church's unease with those aspects of its own message which displease the world. To try to speak of Jesus' distinctiveness as a special revelation of God while not putting him into a category all on his own is seriously to qualify what one is seeking to affirm.

What Peter asserts in Acts 4:12 is endorsed by the New Testament as a whole. He makes clear that it is because of Jesus' name which is 'Christ' that there is no other saviour and consequently no salvation in any other. The word 'other' in Acts 4:12 means 'of a different kind'. Though the existence of numerous saviours may be claimed by the world and that fact is known to the church, there are basically only two kinds: Jesus and all the rest. Because Jesus is the Christ *of God*, the salvation of God is found in him alone. Because he bears the title he does, that is 'Christ', his uniqueness *must* amount to exclusiveness.

Peter was aware of the existence of other religions as was Paul, who referred to the fact that there were many gods and lords who were recognised and worshipped (1 Corinthians 8:5). In saying what he did, Peter therefore knew that Jew and Gentile, with all their sub-groups and differing beliefs and rituals were being excluded. But that was exactly what he wanted to say. Here again, a contradiction must be noted between apostolic Christianity and much of what passes for Christianity at the present time. Peter was at pains to exclude other saviours and other ways of salvation. Today, strenuous efforts are being made to include them, as we shall now see.

This enlargement has been attempted by means of three lines of thought which represent not only shifts of emphasis from the exclusive position adopted by the Christian church but also deviations from basic Christian teaching. They can be set out as follows:

1. A concentration on God in relation to mankind but not on Jesus Christ.
2. A concentration on Christ in relation to the world but not on Jesus of Nazareth.
3. A concentration on the Divine Spirit in relation to the world but not on the Spirit of the Lord Jesus Christ.

Though there is no strict division between these viewpoints, it would not be correct to see them as so many parts of a single theological position. Even so, a certain cross fertilisation does take place between them. They do flow together. To present each of them would take a considerable amount of space and would take us far from the purpose of this book, but something must be said about each as together they form the relevant background to it. A few comments will therefore be offered about each.

1. A Concentration on God in relation to mankind but not on Jesus Christ.

What this approach does is to maximise in a totally non-discriminating way the fact that a reference to deity is common to all religions. In doing this, the uniqueness of the person and work of the Lord Jesus Christ in the matter of salvation, is seriously marginalised or dispensed with altogether.

The late Bishop J. A. T. Robinson, author of *Honest to God* asserted the omnipotence of God's love and claimed that eventually it would win acceptance and response from everyone. But he did not recognise how central and crucial the life and death of the Lord Jesus Christ were as a revelation of that love to the world. Consequently, it was not at all important or necessary that everyone, or anyone, should believe in him. God would win acceptance because his love was omnipotent and not because of Christ's redemptive work.

The strongest Protestant advocate of this God-centered perspective was (and is) John Hick. Using as an analogy, the way in which Copernicus altered thinking about the universe, he contended for a revolution in theological thinking about the relationship between Christianity and World Religions. For Hick, God and not Christ was to be the sun around which all the religions in the world's system revolved, Christianity included. He claimed that a Christ-centred view of things prevented the church from seeing how all religions related to the one God who has many names.

As a direct consequence of this shift, Hick was obliged to engage in a revision of the Church's thinking about Christ, demolishing the traditional view of the eternal and divine sonship of Christ on which the exclusive position was, rightly, seen to rest. He attempted that by means of the volume of essays which he edited, entitled *The Myth of God Incarnate*. It caused a stir in its own day similar to that which Bishop Robinson's book, *Honest to God* had done in the sixties.

2. A Concentration on Christ in relation to the world but not on Jesus of Nazareth

In this approach to other religions, use is made of the statement at the beginning of the gospel of John that the Logos or Christ is the light of men. This is taken to mean that he is present as an enlightening power throughout the universe and in mankind, certainly not only in the church. He is the 'cosmic Christ' and is present in non-Christian religions though in a hidden way. As a result the phrase 'the Unknown Christ' has been coined. Devout adherents to these other faiths are then recognised as 'anonymous Christians' because an implicit faith in God is understood to be present (through Christ) in their hearts.

3. A Concentration on the Spirit but not on Jesus Christ.

From what has been said about one and the same God being present in all religions, it is but a short step to speaking of the one divine Spirit as inditing and inspiring all faiths and worship, including tribal rituals.

Dr. Robert Runcie, the former Archbishop of Canterbury, has made several statements about God being 'the irreducible mystery' present in all forms of worship; 'a higher and stronger power than that of human beings'. But in his lecture on the occasion of the fiftieth anniversary of the World Congress of Faiths he went further and referred to his belief that 'other faiths than our own are genuine mansions of the Spirit'.(capital "S" original).[21]

The Inter-Faith dialogue refers to the way in which the Spirit uncovers to Christians the deepest truths about themselves as human beings and as Christians as they engage in dialogue with people of other faiths and cultures. Salvation is by the Spirit at work in the world apart from Jesus Christ. But is this what Scripture teaches? Will not the Spirit of Truth always convince of sin and lead to Christ (John.16:8ff)?

What would Peter have said if he had been faced with all this? He would simply have repeated for us today what he said in Acts 4:12 where he referred to the one name in which salvation is found. Which name is that? Is it (just) God, or the divine Spirit or the Christ? What is the name of this saviour? Acts 4:10 gives us the answer. It is not just 'God'. Nor is it 'the Spirit'. It is not even just 'Christ'. The name of the saviour is 'Jesus Christ of Nazareth'. It is the Messiah who was Jesus. And not any Jesus, for that was a common name, but a particular Jesus from Nazareth. Salvation is found in history not philosophy; it is found in fact not in mysticism; it is found in a particular individual not in a cosmic being, ineffable deity nor even High Creator God. Just as there is no Christ apart from Jesus the Christ so there is no God apart from the one revealed in Jesus the Christ. God is only personally and savingly knowable through Jesus Christ.

b) Universality

To reject the kind of universalism which is favoured by those who adopt a pluralistic view of truth and accept the saving validity of non-christian religions, and to assert the exclusiveness of Jesus Christ as the only saviour, does not contain any suggestion that Christianity is for some kind of elite. Nor must Christianity ever be thought of as a minority faith. Such conclusions are as forbidden by Scripture as the heresy which is being opposed. No, the good news is for the world and the world needs it. Peter was affirming this when he used the expressions 'under heaven' and 'among men'. The gospel has a worldwide bearing and scope of reference.

By the expression 'under heaven' Peter was referring to the whole earth. No part of the universe is excluded at this point. 'Among men' is a reference to the earth's inhabitants in their number and variety (women and children included) as well as in their common humanity. David Edwards' restriction of Peter's statement to the Jews who were present fails to treat these universalising expressions at all. Associating 'under heaven' and 'among men' and relating them to the matter of salvation means that there is no other saviour in the whole wide world and all the people of the whole wide world need that saviour.

Peter offers two reasons for this universality of the salvation which is in Jesus Christ. They are found in the two words *given* and *must*. The first relates to the single divine provision and the second to the common human need. God has given Jesus Christ and no other to bring his salvation to sinners all over the earth who stand in desperate need of it.

The basic fatal weakness of all 'saviours' other than Jesus Christ is that they are only human and therefore by definition they themselves need saving because they are sinful. Consequently, they are unable to deal with the sin which creates the need for salvation. Salvation cannot come from within the human race. Where then can it come from? It cannot come from the devil because he hates sinners and does not want them to be saved. To worship him, as many are doing, will not provide life. It is only God who has the love and the righteousness and the power to provide it. But he is the one so grievously sinned against and justly angered. Yet he does provide it for sinners and freely ! It is given, sovereignly and graciously, but only in one person, Jesus Christ, and that was incredibly costly. Because that salvation is divine it must be sufficient for the whole world. And all the world needs it. God loves all sinners. 'God so loved the world'. No one can say there is no love for him or her in God and no salvation. Anyone, anywhere, who believes in Jesus Christ, God's Son, will not perish but will have everlasting life.

But will everyone, everywhere, who does not believe in him perish?

What about those who cannot believe because they have never, ever heard? This has become a huge problem and we will concentrate on it in the remainder of this book. We take the liberty of introducing it here because we are dealing with Acts 4:12 and have mentioned the writings of John E. Sanders.

We have already seen that the plain meaning of Acts 4:12 is avoided by many in the wider ecclesiastical scene and the basis on which that is done. It is our conviction that evangelicals ought not to feel vulnerable before such arguments. Peter Cotterell despatches Knitter's treatment of Acts 4:12 for the fabrication which it is. Bracketing it with John 14:6 he writes:

> *'Although these two verses are in a sense isolated verses, they are entirely in accord with the teaching of the New Testament in general. They cannot be dismissed as mere eccentricities. It simply will not do to import into the Bible the modern reluctance to believe in absolutes. We may decide to reject absolutes for ourselves, but we must do that by ourselves and for ourselves. We cannot claim biblical support for our decisions'.*[22]

Now it would be comforting if that were all that we needed to do in order to uphold the traditional understanding of this great verse. But it is not. Sadly, we have to point out what some evangelicals are saying. They are growing in number and Cotterell is included among them. Because they speak as evangelicals they present a far greater threat to the traditional position that it is necessary to believe in Jesus Christ in order to be saved, than Knitter, Hick, and Rahner etc.

These evangelical scholars regard Acts 4:12 as only teaching that salvation is in and by Christ, but no more. They resist explicitly and strongly the view which says that because salvation is in Christ alone, people have to know about him so as to trust him and be saved by him. In their view that is going beyond what this text says.

At this point we turn to what John Sanders who teaches in Oak Hills Bible College, Minnesota has to say about Acts 4:12. Though he acknowledges unreservedly that John 14:6 and Acts 4:12

'certainly teach that any who receive final salvation do so only because of the atonement of Jesus', he writes that:

> '*It is not certain from these passages that one **must** hear of Christ in this life to obtain salvation. They simply say there is no other way to heaven except through the work of Christ; they do not say one has to know about that work in order to benefit from that work*' [23] (emphasis original).

One of the arguments which he presents in support of his case is based on the rules of logic in philosophy. Taking the argument to his opponents he writes:

> '*Furthermore, Romans 10:9 could be summarized as saying "If anyone receives Christ", but this proposition cannot, according to the rules of logic, be converted to read, 'If anyone does not receive Christ, then he is lost'. Again the statement 'All who receive Christ will be saved' is not synonymous with 'All who do not receive Christ will be lost'. The argument, 'If you accept Christ then you will be saved. You did not accept Christ. Therefore, you are lost' is fallacious. There is one sure way of salvation and that is to accept Christ. But these verses do not logically rule out other ways that Christ may save'.*[24]

As it is only Sanders who specifically employs this argument from Logic we will deal with it here. He is claiming that no negative implication can be drawn from Acts 4:12 because it is not cast in the form of a full logical syllogism. The question which may legitimately be asked in reply is whether Holy Scripture is written according to the canons of Logic and is to be regarded as a textbook on that aspect of philosophy. It has long been said, and loudly, that Scripture is not a scientific textbook. That being so, why should it be governed by the rules of Logic?

It is the immediate context of a statement which performs the twin functions of elucidating its meaning and limiting its scope of reference.

The context of Acts 4:12 has already spoken of faith as the means by which the virtue inherent in the Name of Christ is released and made operative in a person's life (3:16). To treat Acts 4:12 as if it were just a general and impersonal statement and not a truth which is related to faith in Christ is therefore to ignore the context. Similarly the emphasis on one name and one only, must exclude all other names.

It is strange that when Sanders comes to a statement which does the kind of thing he says Acts 4:12 does not do, namely follow a positive assertion by a counter-balancing negative one, he finds fault with that as well. We refer to 1 John 5:12 which reads 'He who has the Son has life; he who does not have the Son of God does not have life'. Rather than face up to the fact that the positive is buttressed by the negative, Sanders there invokes the idea of an implicit faith to evade the categorical exclusion in the second part of the statement. But to 'have the Son' (v.12) is to believe God's testimony about him, as the previous verse declares. It is explicit faith which is spoken of.

W.Gary Phillips responds to Sanders on the argument from Logic as follows:

> 'As an illustration (Sanders) cites Rom.10:9 and summarises it thus: "all who receive Christ will be saved". He then invokes the laws of immediate inference from A-Form categorical propositions to say '(this) is not synonymous with "All who do not receive Christ will be lost".' To say so, he avers is 'fallacious'. While this is technically true, language communicates more than categorical propositions. There are semantic nuances which are implied. The parent who says to his child, 'If you clean your room, I'll give you a cookie' means at the same time 'If you do not clean your room, I'll give you a cookie anyway'. Logic may be invoked to serve exegesis, not to exorcise implications'.[25]

Some evangelicals therefore want to uphold the positive assertion of Acts 4:12 without regarding it as containing an implicit negation. We maintain that this is not legitimate contextual interpretation. But in addition, they use two other arguments in support of their view that salvation which is through Christ alone comes to people apart from faith in him. First they deny that all such are liable to condemnation and secondly they assert that at least some of these are actually declared in the Bible to be accepted by God. We consider these in the next two chapters.

From what has been said we can gain a glimpse of what has to be grappled with in the remainder of this book. What we are faced with is not an intentional and explicit rejection of biblical particularism. To claim that would be unfair because those who adopt it would say that they are being more sensitive to larger biblical perspectives and to the limitations of the meaning of particular texts. We must examine their claims in general and particular to see whether their presentation is more in keeping with the whole of Scripture or not. We proceed to that task.

Endnotes

1. P.F.Knitter No Other Name? A Critical Survey of Christian Attitudes Toward World Religions. Maryknoll New York Orbis 1985

2. J.Hick & P.F.Knitter (eds) The Myth of Christian Uniqueness: Toward a Pluralistic Theology of Religions. Maryknoll New York Orbis 1987 / London SCM 1988

3. See his Christianity and the Non-Christian religions in Christianity and Other Religions eds. Hick and Hebblethwaite Fount Collins 1980

4. Broad is the Path. World October 21 1995

5. Declaration on the Relation of the Church to Non-Christian Religions. Vatican Council 11 ed.A Flannery. Fowler Wright. Hereford 1980 p.379

6. Dogmatic Constitution on the Church. Flannery op.cit.p.367

7. No Other Name! Eerdmans Grand Rapids 1992

8. Essentials: A liberal-evangelical dialogue. David L.Edwards & J.R.W.Stott. Hodder & Stoughton 1988 p.298

9. Commentary on Acts of the Apostles. in. loc. Banner of Truth Trust 1963

10. Critical & Exegetical Handbook to the Acts of the Apostles in loc. T.&T.Clark Vol 1 1878

11. Commentary For English Readers in loc. Clarendon Press Oxford 1912

12. Moffatt New Testament Commentary in loc. Hodder & Stoughton 1931

13. Westminster Commentaries in loc. Methuen 1912

14. Clarendon Bible in loc. Oxford 1951

15. Interpreter's Bible in loc.Nashville 1954

16. The Acts of the Apostles in loc. Tyndale Press 1951 & IVP 1990

17. Tyndale New Testament Commentaries in loc.IVP 1980

18. The Message of Acts in loc. IVP 1980

19. New Testament Commentary in loc. Baker 1980

20. Alexander op.cit. in loc.

21. R.Runcie. Christianity and World Religions. World Faiths Insight New series 14 October 1986

22. Cotterell op.cit p.56

23. Sanders op.cit.p.246

24. ibid.p.247

25. Phillips op.cit.p.238

No Condemnation

One of the arguments used to support the case for the salvation of those who have never heard the good news about the Lord Jesus Christ is the claim that all such are not liable to condemnation. We will seek to evaluate that by considering the arguments which Peter Cotterell presents in his book entitled 'Mission and Meaninglessness '. Those arguments are set out by him in the form of Ten Theses with explanatory comments. He intends them to be an answer 'to the questions which are properly raised by an exclusivist missiology'.

His position is being highlighted for two reasons. First, he is the only evangelical in the United Kingdom to argue openly and strongly in print for the position stated. Secondly, given his service on the mission field and position as former Principal of the London Bible College, his writing is likely to be influential in missionary circles.

Of course it was not unforeseen either by Cotterell or the book's publishers that his position would raise questions for evangelicals. The back cover of the book draws the reader's attention to this by saying in a provocative manner that:

> 'It is the first book by a leading British evangelical to recognise God's saving activity among those who live without the church and without an overt knowledge of the gospel. As such, it holds out a special challenge to traditional Evangelicalism, while also having much to say which Christians of all persuasions will find stimulating and refreshing'.[1]

While it is true that the church has recognised that children dying in infancy and those incapable of rational understanding will be saved (see chapter 5), Cotterell is arguing that others beyond these categories will also be saved. An examination of his case is clearly called for because of its potentially harmful effect on missionary activity, evangelistic preaching and witnessing. In addition, the grounds on which he bases his case involve the meaning of Scripture texts. But no thorough examination has to our knowledge yet appeared in print. Comment has been made on particular aspects of it in book reviews but a lengthier treatment is called for. There is so much at stake.

Our method will be two-fold. First, we will consider Cotterell's general approach to the subject. Secondly, the actual arguments on which his contentious claim is based will be examined to see if they can bear the weight put on them.

THE GENERAL APPROACH

It is true that there is much in the book, 'Mission and Meaninglessness' which is not only informative but thought provoking. But while its range of contents is vast and impressive there is need for more detail in the coverage and an overall lack of cohesiveness is noticeable at times. The book resembles a series of lectures more than a single, integrated production.

The combination of the terms 'meaninglessness' and 'mission' in the title is of course deliberate and significant. By 'meaninglessness', the term is borrowed from the NIV of Ecclesiastes, Cotterell represents the 'hebhel' of life which is spoken of in that Old Testament book and also the 'dukhha' of Buddhism. He is therefore referring in two directions at the same time namely to the Bible and the Judaeo-Christian heritage but also to other religious literature and the worldwide religious scene. He sees the term as representing the universal experience of life in a fallen world with all its frustrations, perplexities and injustices. It expresses the awareness that 'things are not what they ought to be'. The sub-title of the book which is 'The good news in a world of suffering and disorder' intimates that a study of Mission which is not detached from the realities of human life is presented in its pages.

But while it is important that a book on Mission should not have a theoretical air about it, that is not the primary thing to be desired. Of greater importance is that its understanding of what the Mission of the Church is about must be true to the Bible, to its nature and to its particular teachings and that in order to do real good to people.

We must therefore look at what Cotterell has to say about the Bible in general and also about certain of its teachings because his confessed aim is to present a biblical position on Mission. In doing so, we remind the reader of the quotation from John Wesley which was included in the opening pages of this book. Part of the explanation for its inclusion was that in it Wesley describes so movingly and, in our judgement, accurately the importance of adopting a proper approach to the Bible and indeed to every theological inquiry.

APPROACH TO THE BIBLE

It is our conviction that Cotterell's approach to the Bible leaves something to be desired. The opening words of Thesis 1 coupled with Thesis 10 indicate that there is something to examine on this score. Cotterell writes:

> 'To any reasonable person it would appear unjust to condemn people to an eternal hell for failing to avail themselves of a medicine of which they have never heard and moreover, of which they could not have heard. Any solution to the problem posed by the continuing existence of vast numbers of those who through no fault of their own have never heard the Good News about Jesus Christ must be formulated so as to take into account the total character of God as revealed in the totality of Scripture: his grace, mercy, patience, justice, holiness, righteousness, love. And such a solution will not, then, outrage common sense and our common ideas of justice. The Lord of all the earth does what is right'.[2]

The underlined words create some unease about Cotterell's view of and approach to Holy Scripture. While Scripture teaching is not irrational, human beings can be and all too often are unreasonable, notwithstanding all their beliefs to the contrary. The basic principle of Cotterell's statements concede too much ground to human reason. In addition, our unease is confirmed by other statements about Scripture which he makes elsewhere in the book. We shall consider these under the headings of Authority and Perspicuity.

The Authority of Scripture

In the chapter of the book entitled 'The Christian World-View'[3] Cotterell deals with what he calls ' The Interpretation Of Texts' . By the plural noun he has in mind what he refers to as 'the special literatures of the world religions' which, of course, includes the Bible. In this sub-section he does not mention the unique character of the Bible in distinction from all other religious books nor its indispensability for understanding the human need and the divine answer which surely is what (true) Mission is all about. Instead, he emphasises 'the general issue of hermeneutics, the science of interpreting text'. Without wishing to demote the importance of interpretation, we must say that the net effect of this section seems to be not only that the Bible is to be studied like every other book, but also that it is nowhere as easy to understand as believers may have thought. A comparison of this with Wesley's approach will show quite clearly that a difference exists here.

He then has a small paragraph which he calls 'The Question Of Reliability' which is concluded with a significant admission:

*'My own understanding starts from an assumption of the reliability of Scripture **properly interpreted**'.*[4] *(emphasis original)*

Two points need to be made here. The first is that Cotterell uses the word 'reliability' and the second is that he speaks about 'interpretation'. We offer a comment about each.

Reliability and Not Infallibility

While the word *reliability* is not unsuitable as a description of Holy Scripture, the word *infallibility* is the time-honoured evangelical term. Cotterell would have known of this. It is equally well known that many evangelical scholars have in the last couple of decades deemed it necessary to use the term *inerrancy* as well as infallibility in order to do justice to the Bible's character. The reason for this was that some scholars who professed a commitment to evangelicalism were weakening the force and narrowing the scope of the term *infallibility* by restricting it to matters of faith and conduct alone and not history etc.

Cotterell may have some good reason for using the word 'reliability' but is it possible that it indicates something weaker even than the contemporary idea of limited infallibility? Later on in the book, he describes the inerrancy question as one which is irrelevant to the real concern of showing that life does make sense in a world of dukhha.[5] We readily grant this is not the first question people ask or the first thing which the church should say to them, but it is not wholly irrelevant to what they need to hear. There is no sense to life in a fallen world if the Bible is not wholly true.

Properly Interpreted

The inclusion of these words, let alone their italicisation, in a sentence which purports to deal with the nature of the Scripture text, further affects whatever cash value this term *reliability* has. What is reliable for Cotterell is not the text itself but a proper interpretation of it. But what is that? More importantly, how can it be known and shown to be an authentic and not an erroneous interpretation? This statement says absolutely nothing about Scripture itself and that is something which evangelicals have always wanted to do. Though they have always been more than ready to recognise that interpreters can and do err, and that to the disadvantage of the Christian message as well as to the detriment of people generally, they have nevertheless deemed it crucial to say something to the contrary about the sacred texts - that they are inerrant or infallible. To fail to do that is to signal that there is nothing objective which has absolute authority to which everything has to conform.

Even when Cotterell goes on to speak about 'The Question Of Truth' by way of concluding this sub-section, he has nothing to say about Scripture being true in fact and meaning.

The Perspicuity of Scripture

Part of the Reformation conviction about the Bible, held by leaders and people, was the belief that Scripture is largely clear to all who read it with faith. Wesley's comments at the beginning are a testimony to this. But Cotterell conveys the message that Scripture is difficult for the ordinary Christian to understand. He becomes explicit on this point by means of an autobiographical reference. (Is this book his farewell to historic evangelicalism?) He writes:

> 'I now realise as I did not thirty years ago that the responsible and accurate interpretation of Scripture is not, in fact, in the hands of the ploughman, and that even the best of translations of the Bible will not make that possible'.[6]

Clearly in Cotterell's reckoning the possession of an accurate translation of the Bible into one's own language coupled with faith, is not enough to make the Bible intelligible. The contribution of biblical scholarship is for him, essential: not simply useful but essential. To think like this is to depart from the doctrine of the Protestant Reformation, with its emphasis on Scripture alone in relation to authority, and Scripture, its own interpreter, in relation to its interpretation. The result is to enthrone an academic elite as interpreters of Scripture in a way which is analogous to the episcopal magisterium of the Roman Catholic church. Nor should the reference to the ploughman be allowed to pass. William Tyndale laboured to put the Bible into the hands of the ploughboy in English. *Surely* this remark is disparaging both to him and to the views which sustained him through life and in death. It is most regrettable, even offensive.

The net effect of this general approach to Scripture is expressed in the words quoted above from the Theses: ' *To any reasonable person it would appear to be unjust..*' and ' *Such a solution will not outrage common sense and our common ideas of justice*'. Though these Theses are an attempt on Cotterell's part to state a biblical position, it will be seen from the above quotations that he lays great emphasis on that position being acceptable to the human mind. The terms he uses in these two places make it quite clear that nothing can be biblical which will not commend itself to the reasonable and the moral. Indeed, what fails to do so cannot be right and true. Human reason is allowed to adjudicate on what is true and false.

Such thinking is out of keeping with many statements in Holy Scripture which give priority to God's word over man's thought and require human beings to submit to and not to alter the words of God. The most emphatic statement of this sort is probably "Let God be true and every man a liar" (Romans 3:4). But, can a single verse be quoted in support of Cotterell's position at this point? We cannot think of one. On what basis then does he assert it?

From the fact that God has revealed himself through 'a written word and through an incarnate Word' he argues that human language, 'does not cease to carry its normal meaning merely because of the irruption of the divine into it'.[7] It therefore follows for him that what is 'just' in human parlance and conduct is what is just, and must be so, for God as well. Man's view of what is just either confirms God's justice or may be allowed to correct it. To declare that God is right and always just, however it may appear to us to be otherwise, is for Cotterell, reminiscent of Islamic teaching about Allah and is 'not the Christian understanding'.

Now, while it is true that human language and divine revelation are not diverse languages - they are found together in Scripture and supremely in Jesus Christ, God's incarnate word - the reality of a divine priority and condescension in all of this must not be overlooked. God has chosen to use human language as an instrument of revelation. Our language has not been imposed upon him. In addition, for him to use our language necessarily involves an act of condescension. While what he has revealed is intelligible and trustworthy, there are things which he has chosen not to disclose (Deuteronomy 29:29). We must therefore think in the opposite direction to Cotterell: we must begin with God and move towards mankind. Though he has come down to us we must always let God be above and beyond us, especially because we have fallen away from him through sin.

Applying all this to the matter of what is just, two things must be remembered. The first is that when the Bible speaks about what is just, it does not endorse what is unjust whether for God or for man. The Bible does not teach with a forked tongue. Secondly, because man is finite and sinful and God is not, his justice must be higher, more perfect than ours, though it might appear to us to be less so. One day his justice will be universally incontestable and he will be seen to have been most just in all that he has said and done. Christians should be content with that now, and should proclaim it and live by it, not trimming it to what is acceptable to us human beings. When that is not done Scripture, God's own word, comes to be subordinated to man's standards and that is serious. Destructive consequences follow for other biblical teachings and for human beings.

THE PARTICULAR ARGUMENTS

We now move on to examine those arguments which Cotterell advances as supporting reasons for his view that people can be saved without their having been evangelised. It is at this point that the Ten Theses become relevant and we therefore print them in full. Cotterell regards them as 'an attempt to state succinctly a biblical position'.

1. To any reasonable person it would appear unjust to condemn people to an eternal hell for failing to avail themselves of a medicine of which they have never heard and moreover, of which they could not have heard.

2. The Passion - the death, resurrection and ascension of Christ - provides sufficient covering for all sin, of all peoples, of all nations and throughout history.

3. *There is a divine self-revelation in creation which is not of itself salvific, but which may lead to the abandoning of human religious effort and to a flight to the mercy and grace of God.*

4. *Those who, in the spirit of Romans 1:21-23 refuse God's self-revelation in creation, and worship the created rather than the Creator, rightly incur the wrath of God.*

5. *Those who have never heard the Christian Good News overtly preached, but who perceive God's eternal power and deity in his creation and seek after him in faith may, by the grace of God, be saved through the passion of that only Saviour of whom, through no fault of their own, they have not heard.*

6. *An individual may be saved in a religion or outside of a religion, but cannot be saved by a religion.*

7. *Salvation comes to us exclusively through Christ, but an overt knowledge of Christ was not a condition of salvation under the Old Covenant and is not a condition of salvation under the New Covenant.*

8. *God's eternal power and divine nature are revealed in creation, and the human apprehension of that power and nature is only made possible through the illumination from the Logos, which shines upon everyone born into the world.*

9. *The Christian Mission is valid because only in an overt knowledge of the Good News about Jesus Christ can we hope to live a truly human and meaningful life now, looking forward with confidence beyond death to the consummation of that purpose for which we were created.*

10. *Any solution to the problem posed by the continuing existence of vast numbers of those who through no fault of their own have never heard the Good News about Jesus Christ must be formulated so as to take into account the total character of God as revealed in the totality of Scripture: his grace, mercy, patience, justice, holiness, righteousness, love. And such a solution will not, then, outrage common sense and our common ideas of justice. 'The Lord of all the earth does what is right'.*[8]

Cotterell presents these as ways of 'thinking and doing Mission'. This means that they are much more than a declaration of personal belief, though they are that. They are intended to have an actual effect on missionary activity. That dimension must be borne in mind in any evaluation of them. It is not enough to ask whether the claims are biblically accurate, consideration must also be given as to what their effect is likely to be. Do they, at least potentially, have an harmful effect on missionary activity and evangelistic preaching and witnessing, or the reverse? What will be the bearing on the financial support of missionary societies?

Given the striking nature of Cotterell's position vis-a-vis the unevangelised, it is important to realise what he is not saying. He makes it quite clear that he is neither a pluralist like Hick, who advocates that there are many ways to one God, nor an inclusivist like Rahner and Kung, who declare that the church or the cosmic Christ includes people from all religions, unknown to them, within the fold. (see Chapter 2). For Cotterell, salvation is only through Jesus Christ. (see Theses 2,5, and 7) Referring to Christ he declares 'No other way needs to be found; no other way can be found'. It is the atonement of Jesus Christ which is sufficient for all as for one. Cotterell is also clear that salvation is by grace (Thesis 5) and that there is something real and awful to be saved from, namely the wrath of God (Thesis 4). With regard to the latter, he distances himself from the notions of Conditional Immortality and Annihilation which are becoming increasingly popular among evangelicals. We do not propose to comment on each Thesis in turn but rather to gather from them the main supporting arguments for the position that salvation will be extended to at least some who have never heard of the Lord Jesus Christ. In our view, four arguments need to be taken into account, which we will consider in turn. They are:

1. It would be unjust of God to condemn those who have never heard of Jesus Christ. (Thesis 1)

2. By means of General Revelation, God points them toward salvation. (Thesis 3)

3. The Logos illumines them. (Thesis 8)

4. God will graciously hear a cry for mercy, made in faith, without the
   suppliant ever having heard of Jesus Christ. (Thesis 5)

1. IT WOULD BE UNJUST OF GOD TO CONDEMN THEM

In his expansion of Thesis 1 Cotterell declares:

> 'That they have never heard of Jesus the Messiah is due
> not to a failure on their part, as if they were to seek him,
> but to a failure on the part of the church which is
> commanded to seek them'.[9]

After pointing out that an overt knowledge of Christ is just not
obtainable unless the church undertakes and performs its duty,
Cotterell writes:

> 'A soteriology which insists on the necessity of such an
> overt knowledge (of Christ) must necessarily condemn all
> these myriads to an eternal separation from God'.[10]

Two main points need to be made by way of reply to Cotterell's moral
and emotional indignation. First of all we must comment briefly on the
emotional reaction which lies just beneath the surface of Cotterell's
words. Those who take the view which Cotterell rejects can easily be
pilloried as heartless. But the fact of the matter is that very many people
have gone to the mission field intending to live and die there precisely
because they believed that people needed to hear the gospel in order to
escape condemnation and be saved. They were 'exclusivists'- but they
went. No one should feel easy about dealing with this matter while he or
she has no heartfelt concern for the condition and destiny of unevangelised people. But compassion for lost mankind and the moral high
ground is not the peculiar preserve of those who take Cotterell's
viewpoint.

Emotional factors, however, are not the basis on which this question
is to be settled. It must be determined by the teaching of Scripture. We
therefore turn to the moral/doctrinal objection which Cotterell
expresses so strongly in Thesis 1, that it would be unjust of God to

condemn those who have never heard the gospel.

In fact many will not feel the force of Cotterell's argumentation at this point because they actually have never thought that the Bible teaches that people are condemned *because they have not heard the Gospel.* They would be ready to agree with Cotterell that if it did, then God would be acting unjustly in condemning them. They believe that the basis or moral ground on which people are liable to condemnation is their own sinfulness and that it is not unjust of God to condemn them on that *account.* So in spite of the vigour with which he presents it, Cotterell's thesis to them is a paper tiger.

But this matter is not disposed of as easily as someone who makes the above rejoinder may think. This is because Cotterell knows the reply to his position which has been summarised above and even though it has been presented by noteworthy missionary colleagues, he is unmoved by it. He refers by name in this precise connection to writings by J. Oswald Sanders and Dick Dowsett quoting the latter as having said 'The unevangelised do not die because they are unevangelised but because of their sin'. Having quoted those words, Cotterell responds immediately by saying:

> '*But this merely pushes back the argument one further step. The unevangelized are condemned because of their sin, but since they have not heard of Christ they have no remedy for it and indeed, no adequate understanding of it. Their condemnation is* **still** *because they have not been evangelized'.*[11] *(emphasis original)*

A confusion exists here. It results from the fact that Cotterell insists on making a connection where in fact a distinction is called for. He speaks of 'taking the argument back' and so proceeds to connect sin with not being evangelised. The basis on which he does this is that being evangelised makes known not only the remedy for sin but also something of its nature, both of which an unevangelised person does not know. For Cotterell, being evangelized provides the basis and standard of being justly judged because apart from it, sin is not even perceived for what it is.

Is this what Scripture teaches? Must judgment be unjust if it falls where the gospel has not been disseminated? That is what Cotterell is affirming. But what about those people who died between Eden and Sinai (see Romans 5:12), to whom no promise nor command had been personally made known? The apostle Paul did not seem to question the justice of their being judged.

It is a distinction which is called for at this point and not a connection. Being evangelised must not be allowed to enter into the sin-judgment relationship as far as the unevangelised are concerned. Sin exposes the sinner to judgment, irrespective of whether the message of salvation is or becomes known. Ignorance of sin's sinfulness is part of sin's entail and it is culpable. It is not attributable to lack of gospel preaching.

Dowsett connects human sin and receiving some divine revelation as the basis on which, and the standard by which, one is justly judged. The liability of all to condemnation is just. It is the variation in the degree of punishment which takes account of the differences in privileges received. Hearing the gospel is a privilege and not a right, though making it known to all is a Christian duty. The gospel not only offers salvation genuinely to all, it also increases the responsibility and penalty of those who hear it but refuse to believe. But judgment is not suspended on whether the gospel is heard or not.

To make Cotterell's connection therefore breeds confusion, whereas the distinction has a clarifying effect. This is highlighted by the different ways in which Cotterell and Dowsett seem to use the preposition 'because' in the quotations given above. Dowsett uses the term strictly to point to the moral ground on which a sentence is carried out. Cotterell uses it, loosely, with more of the meaning of 'by way of result of'.

Of course, what needs to be brought into Cotterell's discussion is mankind's relationship to Adam, to his sin and to his guilt. However, he makes no reference to Romans 5:12-21 in the Theses or in their expansion. By this omission Cotterell does not do justice to the position which he dismisses.

Later in the book, in a chapter entitled 'The Human Disorder' he does refer to that passage and to verse 12 in particular where Paul says that death came into the world through Adam's sin. He notes that 'two possible explanations' exist of the connection between Adam's sin and 'human sin and death' The first is that Adam's sin let loose a spirit of rebellion throughout mankind. This we may describe as original sin. Cotterell states that he is content with that understanding and so declares the other explanation to be superfluous though he records it. It is that 'Somehow the consequences of Adam's sin, the sentence of death, passed upon us all because we all, in Adam, share the guilt'.[12]

This means that Cotterell accepts the doctrine of original sin but not of original guilt which is the imputation of Adam's sin to all his posterity, rendering them guilty before God. But this alternative understanding is not only possible as an exegesis of 'because all sinned' or 'in whom all sinned' in Romans 5:12, it is clearly required by the analogy which is presented and developed between Adam and Christ in the larger context. Sinners are declared guilty by God in the same basic way that they are declared righteous before God which is by imputation: the former on the basis of Adam's sin and the latter on the basis of Christ's obedient work.

This understanding which Cotterell dismisses out of hand is, of course, fatal to his view that those who have not heard the gospel cannot be judged. They are judged already and are liable to condemnation already - on the basis of Adam's sin.

2. BY MEANS OF GENERAL REVELATION, GOD POINTS THEM TOWARDS SALVATION

This argument is related to more than one of the Theses. We begin with Thesis 3 in the expansion of which Cotterell makes reference to Romans 1:18-32, Acts 17:22-34 and John 1:9. As the latter verse is the single text which provides the next argument to be considered, we will postpone treatment of it. It is to be noted that Cotterell excludes the case of Cornelius recorded in Acts 10 and we will consider later why he does that and what Pinnock has to say about that chapter.

We therefore have Romans 1:18-32 and Acts 17:22-34 to examine.

Cotterell's claim that both passages refer to General Revelation, though the first deals with condemnation and the second (arguably) with salvation, can be accepted. It is a pity that the Romans 1 passage, which on Cotterell's admission deals with condemnation, was not taken into account by him in relation to his claim in Thesis 1. As we have pointed out, it has something relevant to say.

In his expansion of Thesis 1 he declares that General Revelation consists of 'the threefold witness of conscience, the witness of God's self-revelation in creation, and the witness of some more or less defective religion'.[13] General Revelation is a descriptive theological term for God's self-revelation to people of all nations, that is the meaning of the adjective 'general', as distinct from Special Revelation which is his self-revelation to some. There is another difference between the two which is relevant to the subject in hand which we will consider later. But both what is general and what is special are revelation: each is a divine activity of self-disclosure.

Given that fact, the question needs to be raised as to whether Cotterell is correct or wise in including 'religion' in General Revelation. We are not suggesting that there is no truth whatsoever in these religions. What we are highlighting is that religion is a response (of some kind) to revelation rather than a part of God's self-revealing activity. It is a human construct rather than a divine activity. To include it in the category of General Revelation is again to make a 'logical' connection at a point where a theological distinction ought to be made and it creates confusion.

How then can it be claimed that there are truths in these religions if religion is not part of General Revelation? The answer to this is quite straightforward. It is that those truths are part of God's self-revelation in the created universe and in the moral constitution of all his creatures. The raw material, so to speak, is revelation; religion, the finished article, is woven on the warped loom of rebellious human thinking and desires. This is what is clearly taught in Romans 1:21-23. Cotterell recognises this in Theses 4 and 6.

As has been mentioned, Cotterell admits that Romans 1:18-32 is related to the theme of condemnation and not of salvation. What he has to do in order to bring this passage more on-side, as far as his view is concerned, is to find some way of restricting its scope of reference so that it does not apply to all. That is what he does in Thesis 4 which declares:

> 'Those who in the spirit of Romans 1:21-23 refuse God's self-revelation in creation and worship the created rather than the Creator, rightly incur the wrath of God'.[14]

That sounds acceptable until we ask to whom exactly is he referring? Is it to all or only to some? In expanding this thesis Cotterell makes clear that it does not apply to all. He writes:

> 'The fourth thesis has nothing at all to say about the position of those who, for whatever reason, are not aware of God's self-revelation in creation and are never brought to the point of hearing the good news'.[15]

This demands a firm response. Is there anyone, anywhere, anytime since the Fall, however deprived or oppressed he or she may be, who lacks the awareness of deity and personal accountability which general revelation gives? Everyone has a mental-moral perception from God and about God which has a bearing on themselves. It is crucial that this is not lost sight of, because it means that everyone has a minimum standard to live up to and by which he or she will be judged. The only alternative to accepting this liability to condemnation is to claim that human ignorance is not culpable. Cotterell does not make this claim explicitly but his other arguments tend in that direction.

So far we have considered Cotterell's denial of universal condemnation which we have seen to be related to the two arguments that multitudes have not heard the gospel (special revelation) and that many of these have not been aware of the light of general revelation either. This must add up to a claim that there are some human beings who are totally destitute of all revelation from God! Does Scripture teach that? It does not. The notion ought therefore to be rejected and the reality of a universal awareness of accountability coupled with a fear of condemnation should be endorsed by all evangelicals. It is this that provides evangelistic preaching with a point of reference and contact in every hearer.

But what about the basis on which Cotterell argues that some will be saved without their having heard the gospel? We now proceed to probe the basis on which he makes this claim and do so by means of Thesis 3 which declares:

> *'There is a divine self-revelation in creation which is not of itself salvific, but which may lead to the abandoning of human religious effort and to a flight to the mercy and grace of God'.*[16]

As has already been mentioned, Cotterell makes use of Acts 17:22-34 in support of this claim. He regards this passage as presenting a real connection between general revelation and salvation, though general revelation by itself cannot convey the knowledge which is necessary for salvation. However, he sees verse 27, which declares that human beings "should seek God, in the hope that they might feel after him and find him" (RSV), as ' a clear statement of the salvific purpose of God'.[17]

It is true that, in the course of his evangelistic preaching at Athens, Paul refers to the benevolence of the sovereign God, the creator and governor of all he has made, who desires his human creatures to seek and find him. But it is possible to over-emphasise this general revelation to all and Cotterell does that in several ways.

First, he overdraws the contrast between Romans 1:18-32 and Acts 17:22-34 by making no reference to the fact that the world will be judged in righteousness (Acts 17:31). *Surely* the implication of saying that the world will be judged in righteousness is that the world of mankind is held accountable for its unrighteousness. This is an echo of Romans 1 & 2.

Secondly, his chosen translation of Acts 17:27 is faulty. Something is omitted from Luke's inspired precis of Paul's preaching on this occasion - the word 'perhaps' or some such term. The RSV omits it unjustifiably and Cotterell chooses to overlook it as well. Conrad Gempf who is Senior Lecturer at the London Bible College offers the following more literal translation of verse 27 : 'They should seek after

God, as if perhaps they might grope around to find him, even though he is not far from each of us'.

On this basis and the general context Gempf comments most helpfully:

> *'Paul's statement that God's intention is that people would seek him and perhaps reach out for him and find him , though he is not far from each one of us, might look as though the pagan has only to reach out and touch God. In fact, the language is that of tragedy. The grammar reinforces that this is God's wish, rather than what happens. The word used for the 'seeking' is a very graphic one often translated 'groping' in the sense of 'blindly feeling about for'. The negative result is clearly seen in the final clause : "though he is not far" rather than "since he is not far". The point being made is not 'he is close so people can find him' but rather 'people cannot find him, but that isn't because he is far away".* [18]

Howard Marshall regards the term 'grope after' as possibly expressing 'the sinful failure of man to find God to which Romans 1:20ff point'.[19]

Cotterell's treatment of this verse is therefore too optimistic by far. The meaning of the term 'perhaps' just cannot be avoided. But it is vital to locate it in the proper place. There is no 'perhaps' in God's desire to be sought and found, nor about his nearness to and interest in all his creatures. The reservation or hindrance is whether people will seek and find. In spite of the fact that, as Cotterell says, God has designed the world for human habitation and ordered the seasons so that human life can be supported, many will not seek him who gives everyone life and breath and everything else.

Thirdly, the latter part of Thesis 3 describes the human reaction envisaged as a consequence of General Revelation. Whether the two actions identified there as an 'abandonment' and a 'flight' are intended by Cotterell to bear some resemblance or not to repentance and faith, it is difficult to say. If they are, then surely some mention of sin would have been required in the formalised Thesis. Of more concern is the fact that Cotterell envisages the possibility of 'a flight to the mercy and grace of God' as a result of the light of General Revelation.

In expanding this, Cotterell speaks of 'an existential encounter with God through his creation' which produces an awareness of sinfulness and powerlessness and an acknowledgment of his justice in condemnation with the result that people can be 'flung back on God's grace'. Our difficulty with this does not lie in recognising whether or not something of this kind may occur. It does occur and Job 33:14-22 seems to speak of the very thing. A longing for the God who is and a dissatisfaction with all other so-called gods may arise. The problem lies in how anyone can learn that God is gracious and merciful to sinners from the light of general revelation alone. Benevolent, yes, even beneficent: but gracious-No! This belongs to special revelation. Job 33:23 speaks of the need of a messenger to declare God's righteousness to the sinner.

Before leaving this Thesis one detailed correction must be included. It relates to the expression 'fly to God for mercy'. On page 48 Cotterell writes: 'There is a real experience of God in which, to use the phraseology of Martyn Lloyd-Jones, we "fly to God for refuge". The impression which is given by this attribution is that Lloyd-Jones uses this expression in the same sense as he does. That this is not so is made clear in an end-note by Cotterell in which the actual statement of the Doctor is given in full. It contained an explicit reference to Christ.[20] The record must be set straight on this point.

4 THE LOGOS ILLUMINES THEM

It is Thesis 8 which presents this argument and its use of the Greek term 'logos' is attributable to the fact that Cotterell is concentrating on John 1:9 at this juncture. In the Prologue to John's gospel, that is the first eighteen verses, the term logos which means 'word' is central to all that is said. It refers to the Lord Jesus Christ. What verse 9 focuses on is the Word's enlightening activity.

Cotterell has been arguing that it is possible that someone might be constrained to call on God as a result of general revelation and his experience of life in a fallen world. But he acknowledges in the comment on this Thesis that 'no reliable guide to the nature of God' exists in human thought and conduct, whether religious or secular. The outlook is therefore distinctly discouraging. It is with reference to this state of affairs that he introduces this argument about the illumination of the Logos. He writes:

> 'But we are not left without recourse. John 1:9 is our assurance that there is such a thing as a true light, and that this one true light shines upon us all'.[21]

John 1:9

We turn therefore to a consideration of John 1:9. To do this we have to begin on the level of its translation. As is well known, some disagreement exists as to whether the phrase 'coming into the world' refers to 'every man' or to 'the true light'. The preponderance of contemporary scholarly opinion is in favour of the latter association (see NIV) though the other view (see KJV) has not completely disappeared. (see NIV footnote)

Important though it is, from the standpoint of our inquiry it is not a crucial point : if we adopt the NIV rendering 'the true light was then coming into the world', his enlightening activity is still extended to every human being. The real question at issue relates to the nature of this enlightening and its relationship to other passages of Scripture. These questions are too large to be investigated thoroughly here. What is called for is an evaluation of Cotterell's view on John 1:9 and related passages. That is what we will attempt.

Cotterell links John 1:9 with Romans 1:18-3:18 and Acts 17: 22-31 in the following way. John 1:9 speaks definitively of salvation for some as a result of the enlightenment of the Logos with respect to God as he revealed himself through creation. (Romans 1:19). The rest of Romans 1 and 2 do not deny this possibility because they are not concerned with salvation but condemnation. They are therefore, in the strict sense, beside the point. Acts 17 confirms John 1:9 because it connects General

Revelation quite specifically with God's saving will.

Over against this synthesis, is what we have just shown, that Acts 17 is negative, not positive, in terms of man's response and that the Romans passages speak of condemnation as co-extensive with the human race. It is related to those who receive General Revelation only, as much as to those who receive more. So at this point it can at least be said that Cotterell has not established his position on these passages. But what of John 1:9, the text which is arguably the foundation on which Cotterell's whole position rests?

If it can be shown that there is another interpretation of John 1:9 which is at least as good as the one Cotterell advances and that it also integrates the three passages mentioned above more harmoniously, then we may with justification claim that Cotterell's case has been answered even if it has not been disposed of.

In the course of the church's history this verse has been interpreted in a number of different ways and Cotterell shows awareness of that fact. Two questions need to be faced with regard to its exegesis. The first of these is a watershed. It is the issue whether the enlightening spoken of in this verse refers to a significant revelatory event in time and space or to an intellectual awareness in every human being. Is it objective or subjective. In other words, does it take place externally in the world or internally in every human being who is born into the world?

Cotterell takes the latter view. Many before him have also done that, but they have not all done so in the same sense as he does. This takes us into the realm of our second question. Noting that verse 9 precedes a statement about rejection and acceptance of the Logos after he has come into the world, Cotterell says:

> 'It seems that John is here positing a general **Logos** illumi-
> nation affecting everyone, but not an irresistible illumi-
> nation. But neither is it an ineffective illumination' [22]
> (emphasis original).

In answer to the question as to how it was that some received him, Cotterell replies that it was through that same universal but not irresistible illumination. This means that some will receive the Logos who came into the world but without knowing that he has come and why.

In the course of commenting on John 1:9 Cotterell acknowledges that one modern commentator on John's gospel, C.K.Barrett, no less, denies that the enlightening refers to anything internal at all. He regards it as a 'crisis' event which reveals a person for 'what he is'. Cotterell claims that Barrett is 'in a minority of one' in this view. That is dismissive and inaccurate. Other evangelical New Testament scholars e.g. F.F. Bruce[23], R.V.G.Tasker[24], G.R. Beasley-Murray[25] and Leon Morris[26] do not treat Barrett's exegesis so disdainfully and Don Carson[27] decidedly favours it.

The grounds on which this objective interpretation rests are worth mentioning because they are not as outlandish as Cotterell infers. First, there is the lexical meaning of the verb. Barrett and Carson point out that its primary meaning is 'to make visible' or 'shed light on'. 'To illuminate (internally)' is only the secondary meaning. So what is being described is the coming of light in the person of Jesus Christ, into the world which is in darkness without him.

Secondly, and more importantly, this exegesis fits neatly into the movement of the Prologue and is also confirmed by the subsequent gospel record. Prior to verse 6 which introduces the ministry of John the Baptist, the Prologue deals with Creation and the era which preceded the incarnation of the Word, which is in view in verse 9 and following. The expression of light 'coming into the world' is used frequently in the gospel record and always with regard to the coming of Jesus and the two contrasting responses to him. (see John 3:19-21; 8:12; and 9:39-41) That is the case with John 1:10-13. Barrett writes that the words 'the world knew him not' in verse 10 prove that 'There is no natural and universal knowledge of the light'. He writes:

> 'The function of light is judgment; when it shines, some come to it, others do not. It is not true that all men have a natural affinity with the light'.[28]

Carson agrees and writes:

> 'In John's gospel it is repeatedly the case that the light shines on all, and forces a distinction'.[29]

This objective interpretation is neither forced nor far-fetched. It is quite natural to the terms of the verse and to its immediate and larger contexts. What we conclude therefore is that instead of regarding everyone as being enlightened by the Logos at or in association with their entry into the world, John 1:9 refers to the fact that the entry of the Logos into the world shows whether a person is in the light or in the darkness.

But how does this interpretation sit or square with the Acts and Romans passages which have been referred to? In our view, it harmonises with them much better than Cotterell's subjective view does. We will now try to show that this is so.

John 1:9 provides, as we have seen, the background for the two responses of the rejection and the reception of the light of life which are found in verses 10-13. But if that is so, how can the verse relate to the universal knowledge mentioned in Romans 1:20 ff and Acts 17: 23ff? The answer to that disagreement is that it is John 1:4 and 5 where the Word is described as 'the light of men' which refers to that universal knowledge, and not John 1:9. We therefore have a natural progression in the Prologue where verses 4 and 5 relate to the era which preceded the incarnation of the Son of God, verses 6 and 7 to the ministry of John the Baptist and verses 8 and 9 to the Incarnation and following.

5. GOD WILL GRACIOUSLY HEAR A CRY FOR MERCY, MADE IN FAITH, WITHOUT THE SUPPLIANT EVER HAVING HEARD OF JESUS CHRIST

Theses 5, 6, and 7 present this assertion. Here we have Cotterell's bottom line, the conclusion from all that has gone before. What generates such a cry, in his reckoning, is a combination of three factors. First, there is the enlightening of the Logos which is universal. Secondly, there is the self-revelation of God in creation which is also universal. Thirdly, there is the experience of life's meaninglessness which can vary in intensity or degree depending on social or contextual factors but which is nowhere totally absent. These can give rise to a faith in God that is expressed in a cry to him which he will hear and answer favourably.

So that Cotterell's position might not be misunderstood, two negations need to be made quite unambiguously. First, he emphasises that the cry is made in *faith* and *for mercy*. He is not teaching salvation by works of any kind, least of all by the sincerely held belief and devout practice of any religion. Thesis 6 could not be clearer on that score. It reads:

> '*An individual may be saved in a religion, or outside of a religion, but cannot be saved by a religion*'.[30]

Secondly, Cotterell is not teaching a salvation apart from Christ and his cross. With equal clarity he asserts that the salvation which is not by works is on the basis of and by virtue of Christ's passion. Thesis 2 affirms this though it has to be said that, alongside the emphasis on the sufficiency of Christ's death to deal with all sin, there is not an explanation of the nature of the atonement at this point. Instead Cotterell explicitly avoids doing that. The opening words of Thesis 7 which are 'Salvation comes to us exclusively through Christ...', backed up by John 14:6, again make it clear that he is not talking about a salvation apart from Christ.

Given these welcome assertions it may be wondered how Cotterell can present the conclusion which we are now considering. A clue is found in his comment on John 14:6 which reads:

> '*What this logion (saying of Jesus) does affirm is that in so far as anyone approaches God, that approach is made possible by Christ. There is no other way. What the saying does **not** do is to define the prerequisites of the approach*'.[31] *(emphasis original)*

It is this loophole which enables him to disconnect 'a grace-given faith in God' as Creator from 'an overt knowledge of Christ', pointing to the Old Testament period when people believed in God but could have no knowledge of the incarnation. Thesis 7 therefore declares:

> '*...an overt knowledge of Christ or of the work of Christ was not a condition of salvation under the Old Covenant and is not a condition of salvation under the New Covenant*'.[32]

In expanding this Cotterell rightly remarks that the Epistle to the Hebrews makes it perfectly clear that 'the Old Covenant was of itself unable to deal with sin'. He concludes from this, and from the fact that John 14:6 is 'given without qualification', taking no account of the differences between the Old and New Testaments, that there is only one way of salvation presented in both Testaments. He writes:

> 'The basis of salvation under both covenants, then, was the coupling of the grace of the saving God with the grace-given faith of saved humanity through the work of Christ. The actual nature of the commitment to God was specific to each covenant'.[33]

Because he argues that there was 'no overt knowledge of Christ ... under the Old Covenant' but 'a grace-given faith in God' he can make from that a direct connection with those who have not heard of Christ and say that, potentially, they are in the same position as Old Testament people. But are they? Is that a fair parallel to draw?

In our view the parallel is inaccurate because it pays no attention whatsoever to the existence of Messianic prediction and expectation in the Old Testament period. The Epistle to the Hebrews, which Cotterell quotes in favour of the Old Covenant having no atoning or cleansing efficacy but being weak and unprofitable, is itself full of quotations and allusions regarding the promised Messiah who would accomplish all that the Old Covenant could only foreshadow or typify. Cotterell ignores all that and puts Old Testament people on a par with those who only had the light of general revelation. This will not do as a basis for his claim that an overt knowledge of Christ, who is after all that promised Messiah, is not necessary today because it was (allegedly) not necessary then. It was known then though it existed in embryonic and unfolding form and it was necessary. The parallel does not hold.

A Particular Example

The case of Rahab is mentioned by Cotterell as an example of the kind of faith which saved in Old Testament times and therefore can save today. He quotes from Joshua 2:11 and says that Rahab 'acknowledged God as "(God) in heaven above and on the earth below"'. Consequently, he argues that what is required is:

> '*not* the religious response such as would have had its parallel in Canaanite religion...but the response of faith in the God of Creation, whose eternal power and divine nature was evident'.[34] (emphasis original)

Cotterell has not done justice to Rahab's confession by merely using the words which we have underlined and quoting part of Joshua 2:11. Her declaration of faith begins in verse 9 of Joshua 2 and goes on to verse 13. In what she said she declared 'I know that the LORD...' that is Jehovah, the covenant redeemer of his people with whom she was associating. This is hardly the same response as Cotterell is contending for. The next chapter will focus on other examples of this kind.

One further comment needs to be made. It relates to the example of Cornelius which is documented in Acts 10. Cotterell refers to this but does not use it in support of his case as Pinnock does (see next chapter). This might be surprising, but Cotterell acknowledges that it is 'potentially misleading'. This is because it not only records the case of a seeker but that the seeker was found so that he might be saved. We will show in the next chapter that Acts 10 is not a blunt instrument from Cotterell's point of view; rather, it is too sharp.

Cotterell therefore accepts that what happened to Cornelius may happen to some, but he denies that it has to happen to all if they are to be saved. However, the grounds on which he bases that assertion have proved to be seriously less than adequate. His fall-back position is what has now become the well known incident of Esa. Cotterell writes that Esa 'called on the Gamo people to abandon the worship of their Spirit of Evil, and to worship God'. That took place in Ethiopia in the 1920s. 'When the missionaries finally reached Gamo a decade later they found the people prepared for them, but Esa had died'. Cotterell comments 'It would be strange if they should be saved but their teacher lost...'[35]

What can be said about this? We dare to ask whether it is necessary to say anything - one way or the other? Just as hard cases make for bad law, so strange providences are not for us to plumb, and certainly not for us either to turn into a theology for which there is no substantial evidence or to turn from a theology for which there is. To renounce evil and idolatry is a testimony to the moral dignity of a human being.

In our view, the real evidence which has been presented in this chapter is much more against Cotterell's *cri de coeur* than in favour of it. Of course we feel the poignancy of what he records and do not at all wish to dismiss it out of hand. What he cannot be permitted to do, unchallenged, is to present this plea as if it were a *theological* argument.

The conclusion which we therefore draw from this examination of Cotterell's case is twofold. First, the grounds on which he bases his argument will not, on inspection, bear its weight. Secondly, there is an alternative argument with which he has not come to terms at all and that, we think, has a better claim to be regarded as the biblical position.

Endnotes

1. Cotterell op.cit

2. ibid.p.83

3. ibid. pp.25-35

4. ibid.p.30

5. ibid.p.187

6. ibid.p.167

7. ibid.p.69

8. ibid.pp.75-83

9. ibid.p.75

10. ibid.p.75

11. ibid.p.68

12. ibid.p.109

13. ibid p.75

14. ibid.p. 75

15. ibid.p.77

16. ibid.p.77

17. ibid.p.77

18. New Bible Commentary 21st. Century Edition IVP 1994 p.1094

19. Marshall op.cit in loc

20. Cotterell op.cit.p.284

21. ibid p.81

22. ibid p.63

23. The Gospel of John. Pickering & Inglis 1983. in loc.

24. John. An Introduction and Commentary Tyndale Press 1966 in. loc.

25. John. Word Biblical Commentary. 1987 in.loc.

26 . The Gospel According to John. Marshall, Morgan and Scott 1971 in. loc.

27. The Gospel according to John. IVP 1991. in.loc.

28. Barrett The Gospel According to Saint John SPCK 1965 in loc.

29. Carson op.cit.in.loc.

30. Cotterell op.cit. p.80

31. ibid. p.80

32. ibid p.80

33. ibid. p.80

34. ibid. p.80

35. ibid. p.79

Pagan Saints! —
In the Old Testament

We have shown that some evangelicals argue for the view that people who have never heard the gospel and therefore cannot believe in the Lord Jesus Christ will nevertheless be saved through him. In this chapter we continue our examination of that point of view and now concentrate attention on what is meant by 'pagan saints'.

Clark Pinnock of McMaster Divinity School, Ontario has made a significant contribution to the study of the relationship between Christianity and World Religions. Having outlined some preliminary thoughts in article form, he has recently presented a fully worked out position on this pressing subject. His book, entitled 'A Wideness In God's Mercy', has for its sub-title - ' The Finality of Jesus Christ in a World of Religions'.[1] It is his conviction that the time has come for evangelical theologians to re-appraise their position on this matter and to adopt a more positive approach towards those of other faiths. He claims that the Bible presents such an outlook.

GENERAL APPROACH

As Pinnock's general approach and basic principles are in accord with those of Cotterell, what we have said in chapters 2 and 3 by way of agreement with and dissent from Cotterell is also applicable to the case which he argues. Negatively, Pinnock rejects the thinking of the radicals (Robinson), the pluralists (Hick) and the inclusivists (Rahner and Kung). Positively, he adopts the view which regards General Revelation and the illumination of the Logos as pointing strongly towards the possibility of salvation by means of their light.

He uses a number of texts in support of this positive outlook. In addition to the well known passages in the book of Acts, he refers to Deuteronomy 4:19. This verse explicitly prohibits Israel from worshipping the sun, moon and stars, describing them as ' things which the LORD your God has apportioned to all the nations under heaven'. Pinnock regards this prohibition as applying *only* to Israel but he also deduces from the latter part of the verse that:

'*With liberality Yahweh permitted the nations to worship him in ways not proper for Israel to do*'[2] *(emphasis ours).*

The Deuteronomy text does not require the inclusion of the italicised words to exegete it. There is no suggestion in it that the nations were either worshipping God or that their worship met with divine approval. Pinnock reads that understanding out of the verb 'apportioned' which simply records the fact that in the divine administration of mankind the nations were left to practise idolatry. The same can be said about Pinnock's comment regarding Naaman, namely that his interpretation of II Kings 5:18 goes beyond what Scripture actually says. He comments:

'*God allowed Naaman...to worship in Rimmon's temple because of the delicate circumstances he was in*'[3] *(emphasis ours).*

In point of fact there is no mention in the text of God doing anything. Elisha's words 'Go in peace' do not amount to a divine permission and Naaman himself knew he was doing wrong in what he proposed.

Pinnock also refers to Acts 14:16 and 17:30 in support of his case but they only describe a divine sufferance of the thoughts and ways of the nations and not a saving pursuit of them on the part of God. Pinnock writes:

'*God overlooks the times of human ignorance (Acts 17:30) and passes over former sins (Romans 3:25). Is it possible that we have made God out to appear stingy? Should we not rather be thankful for the wideness of his mercy?*'[4]

He seems to be understanding these verses, certainly the Romans reference, as being tantamount to divine forgiveness, whereas all they declare is that God did not intervene in judgment during the period stated and for the reason given. Postponement of judgment is not the same as pardon for sin.

'PAGAN SAINTS'!

Our main objective in this chapter is to focus attention on one subject area of Pinnock's book. Although it is subsidiary to his main concern, it is by no means unimportant to his case. Indeed, it is, arguably, the corner stone of his argument, and that of others, because of its sustained use of Scriptural data. The title of this chapter and section indicates what the subject area is.

Without the exclamation mark which we have inserted, the title is actually taken from Pinnock's book. A 'pagan saint' is someone who has faith but who is neither a member of the community of Israel nor the Church. He or she is not to be thought of as the equivalent of the 'noble savage' in the romantic and liberal tradition of the nineteenth century in the western world. By his striking juxtaposition of an unusual adjective and noun Pinnock is intending to draw attention to something which, he is convinced, has not generally been recognised in the Bible. He calls it 'the much neglected biblical theme' of 'the holy pagan tradition'. Other writers speak of 'holy pagans', meaning the same thing.

In discussing this 'holy pagan tradition', Pinnock does not dismiss the fact that a deceptive and corrupting influence is exerted in and by many religions, thinking of religions in the objective sense of the term as sets of beliefs and related practices. This he traces in an unambiguous manner to Satan's activity. He does not mince his words on this subject despite the fact that, in the process, he criticises a Christian religiosity as well.

But though he rejects the idea that somehow all religions are valid ways to God, he does say that in the cases of Melchizedek and Jethro, both 'pagan priests', that 'their religions seem to have been vehicles of salvation for them', adding immediately 'But it is not safe to overgeneralise from these cases'.[5] We will consider what is said in the Old Testament about these individuals later.

It is in relation to 'religion' in its subjective sense that he conceives of this holy pagan tradition. He finds it in the existence of 'faith, which is neither Jewish nor Christian, which is nonetheless noble, uplifting and sound'. He gives these examples of it in Scripture :

> 'believers like Abel, Noah, Job, Daniel, Melchizedek, Lot, Abimelech, Jethro, Rahab, Ruth, Naaman, the Queen of Sheba, the Roman soldier, Cornelius and others'.

Of these Pinnock declares:

> '(They) were believing men and women who enjoyed a right relationship with God and lived saintly lives, under the terms of the wider covenant God made with Noah'. [6]

It is our view that what Pinnock says about covenants needs to be examined. We will do so by looking first at how Pinnock relates these 'saints' to a covenantal setting before giving attention to what is actually said about them in the Scripture text. We will divide our treatment into Old and New Testament material.

'PAGAN SAINTS' IN THE OLD TESTAMENT

A foundational passage for Pinnock's entire theological outlook on this matter is found in the following words :

> 'According to the Bible, persons can relate to God in three ways and covenants: through the cosmic covenant established with Noah, through the old covenant made with Abraham and through the new covenant ratified by Jesus. One may even speak of salvation in the broad sense in all three of the covenants. Of course, there is a more complete saving knowledge of God in the new covenant than in the old, and more in the old than in the cosmic covenant, but a

relationship with God is possible in the context of all three covenants. In all three, God justifies Jews and Gentiles on the ground of faith, the condition of salvation in all dispensations' (Rom.3:30).[7]

With Pinnock, we judge it to be a sound biblical principle that people can only relate to God in terms of a covenant which he makes with them. But as this connection needs to be treated in a more careful way than Pinnock does, we will draw attention first of all to what he says about the Abrahamic covenant and the Noahic covenant. We also want to consider a covenant which he does not mention. Having done that we think that we will be in a better position to come to some sort of conclusion about what he says concerning individual pagan saints.

THE ABRAHAMIC COVENANT

Pinnock describes the Abrahamic covenant as 'old' but The New Testament nowhere uses that adjective to describe it. Instead, it denominates the Sinaitic covenant in that way. (Hebrews 8:6-13) The New covenant is the fulfilment of the Abrahamic covenant and not its abrogation. By setting the Abrahamic and the new covenants in such contradistinction from each other Pinnock makes it appear that they exhibit different ways to salvation, which they do not (see Romans 3 and Galatians 3). They are one and the same in essence, in spite of their differences, because they focus on the same promised seed. Consequently, the saints under the Abrahamic and the New covenants are one people, not two.

THE NOAHIC COVENANT

Pinnock places great emphasis on the Noahic covenant in what he has to say about 'pagan saints'. He relates to it all the Old Testament figures whom he names. We have two points to make here. The first concerns the character of that covenant, and the second relates to the time of its disclosure.

The Character of the Noahic Covenant

We do not reject Pinnock's claim that the Abrahamic covenant sets out the same way of faith as the New covenant does, though we would wish to highlight the matter of the promised seed as the specific object of that faith. But we want to challenge what he says about the Noahic covenant. In doing this we are aware that we are falling foul of Pinnock's stricture that:

> '*It is common to interpret the Noahic covenant in a minimalist way and to see it as a covenant only of physical preservation and not of redemption. But surely this is a divine commitment and promise that transcends merely preserving the race from another flood. The promise to Noah prepares the way for the blessing of all nations through Abram a few chapters later. The call of Abram implements the promise made to Noah. Both covenants were universal in scope. For a reader not to see this suggests a hermeneutical presupposition blocking truth out*'.[8]

Pinnock only names Karl Barth in support of his view and it is, at least, arguable that Barth's thinking on this score is coloured by his vigorous opposition to any idea of general revelation or common grace - a vital matter in the whole subject with which we are dealing. But it will be noticed from the quotation that Pinnock has to admit that many take the view of the Noahic covenant which he himself rejects. It is that view which is being advocated in these pages.

To call this view 'minimalist' is to use a tendentious term. In fact, all that Pinnock has to say by way of counter to it is that a connection exists between the Noahic and Abrahamic covenants. But we reply that those who see the Noahic covenant as being limited to 'physical' matters - that is to the earth, its seasons, and a fresh beginning for mankind would not dispute the existence of such a link.

Indeed, they would argue that a close relationship exists between those covenants which can be set out in the following way. The Noahic covenant guarantees a stable universe, free from any threat of a global cataclysmic judgement such as the Flood was, even though sin continues to be practised in it. In such a world the gracious purposes of the Abrahamic and New covenants, and the promises made earlier in Genesis 1-5 are worked out throughout time and among all the nations. The view therefore which Pinnock rejects finds no difficulty in recognising and acknowledging a continuity between the Noahic and the Abrahamic Covenants which is not merely one of time sequence but also of coherence of truths presented.

We think that Pinnock fails to see the important distinction between the Abrahamic and the Noahic covenants and that might equally be said to be the result of 'a hermeneutical presupposition, blocking truth out', to use his own words. But the fact is that no way of salvation for all flesh was made known through the Noahic covenant and no promise of a seed to come was made known to Noah as there would be to Abraham. Pinnock is therefore not correct when he says that

> 'God announces **in this covenant** that his saving purposes
> are going to be working, not just among a single chosen
> nation but among all peoples sharing a common ancestry
> in Noah' (emphasis ours).[9]

It is difficult to see how Genesis 6:18-9:17, the passage which records the Noahic covenant, can be understood in this way. It is quite clearly reminiscent of the Creation narrative in Genesis 1. Abounding sin threatened all that had been made. The Flood was God's way of beginning a new universe and a new humanity, though within the context of the Fall. Genesis 9:25-27 does have something to do with the outworking of God's saving purposes among humanity but that is not the Noahic covenant.

The only knowledge about God which could be gained from that covenant was that God was a preserver of and provider for the life of all kinds of creatures in spite of his being a most awesome judge of the sin of human beings. The fact that the deliverance of eight people from the Flood is referred to later in Scripture (see Isaiah 54:9 and 10 and 1 Peter 3:20-22) as a type of messianic salvation is beside the point. The matter at issue is what people might have come to know as they reflected on the event of the deluge and its immediate aftermath and not what could be learned from subsequent revelation about it.

It is therefore our view that Pinnock makes two general mistakes. The first is that he does not correctly inter-relate the three covenants which he specifies. The second is that he regards his 'pagan saints' as having learned more from the Noahic covenant than was actually possible. We will take up the question of where they could have obtained their knowledge when we mention a covenant which Pinnock overlooks.

THE TIME OF ITS DISCLOSURE

Pinnock makes a major blunder when he says that all his 'pagan saints' 'lived saintly lives under the terms of the wider covenant made with Noah'. That could only be true if the Genesis record were itself untrue as it records that some of them lived before the Flood, for example Abel and Enoch. They could not therefore have lived under the terms of the Noahic covenant. This might also be true of Job and of the Daniel who is mentioned in Ezekiel 14 and 28. In addition, Noah himself had a relationship with God before he began to build the ark. The biblical chronology requires that some differentiations be made between the knowledge of those whom Pinnock groups in the category of 'pagan saints' and a question arises as to where those in the group who lived before the Flood obtained their believing knowledge from. Plainly, it could not have come from the Noahic covenant. From where then could it have come?

PAGAN SAINTS BEFORE THE FLOOD

Pinnock's view is that three covenants have to be considered in relation to God's dealings with human beings. These are the Noahic, the old (Abrahamic) and the new. Though we agree with him that a knowledge of God is only possible as a result of a covenant arrangement through which God discloses himself, we do not agree that there are only three covenants to be reckoned with in this regard. If some 'pagan saints' antedated the time of Noah we must go back further in biblical history in order to evaluate their knowledge. Not only must the first eleven chapters of Genesis, which Pinnock describes as having been neglected, be considered but, more narrowly, the first six of those chapters which are so distrusted.

Attempting to do this, we note that Pinnock speaks of a 'covenant of creation' or 'a cosmic covenant' by virtue of which 'the whole world and its peoples belong to God'. In addition, although he refers once to a covenant made with Adam, he declares that it was also made with Noah. The sentence in which he does that is:

> *'The covenant made with Abram has to be interpreted in the context of the covenant made with Noah and with Adam'.*[10]

Perhaps the singular noun 'covenant' at the end of the sentence should have been in the plural. If we read 'covenants' it would be possible to say that Pinnock recognises that a distinct covenant was made with Adam but as the sentence stands that is not possible. Though Pinnock does refer to Adam as the representative head of all humanity, he does not recognise that a distinct covenant was made with him as such. There does not therefore seem to be to Pinnock anything which is worth noting in that connection as he does not have anything at all to say about the content of God's self-revelation to Adam and Eve.

Pinnock does not examine the first three chapters of Genesis at all and that is surely a serious omission. They are foundational and have relevance to all biblical subjects and particularly to the 'covenant' or binding arrangement made with Adam, the representative head of the entire human race. We will review what we believe to be the relevant data.

In Genesis 1:28 and 2:15-17 we have the record of mankind's duty to God together with the threatened penalty for disobedience to a specific precept. Genesis 3 records the transgression of Adam and Eve and the effects of that. This awareness of living in God's world as his subjects and of being exposed to death on account of sinful rebellion is the background for the Noahic covenant and for those passages in both Testaments which deal with General Revelation. A point of reference is thus provided, as we shall see, for part of the knowledge of some of these 'pagan saints'.

But we want to argue that there is a verse in Genesis 3 which is the background to the Abrahamic covenant and to all the subsequent saving self-disclosures of God. It is, of course, verse 15, which promises a male descendant of Eve who would crush the serpent's (Satan's) head though at the cost of having his own humanity (heel) crushed in the process. This has been regarded as the first proclamation of the gospel, the protevangelium. That promise of a coming seed is something which Adam and Eve believed.

Adam confessed this faith by renaming his wife. He had given her the name 'woman' to indicate her oneness with him as human. The name speaks of creation. Calling her Eve (3:20), a word which comes from the Hebrew for 'to live', is expressive of God's promise to deal with the death which has been introduced through sin. In turn, Eve did something similar by her naming of their sons. Cain (4:1) which means 'obtained' is linked with 'the LORD' and expresses Eve's belief that the promised seed has already come. Seth (4:25) which means 'appointed' is a replacement for Abel and his birth is a testimony to God's faithfulness to his promise over against the malignity of the seed of the serpent. What is more, it is that knowledge of God which we can assume informed the faith of Abel, Enoch and Lamech, the father of Noah (see 5: 28&29). They were all of the line of Adam-Seth and not Cain-Lamech and were looking for the one who would undo what sin had done.

Given this information, they should not therefore be classified as 'pagan saints' at all, but as belonging to the line which was the precursor of Israel and the church. They were saints who were not pagans because saving revelation had been made known to them. To call them 'pagan' saints is to deny that they had received any such saving revelation. They must therefore be removed from Pinnock's list.

Genesis 4:26b ought also to be given due weight, even though one would like to have more information about what it refers to. Literally it means 'Then began to call on the name of the LORD'. An impersonal subject noun needs to be supplied in order to complete the sense e.g. 'people'. Taking this statement at its face value, it records a public and corporate confession of faith in Yahweh (Jehovah), made in the context of the worship, which occurred in the days of Enosh, Seth's son. It stands in marked contrast to the arrogant self-exaltation of Lamech which is expressed in the previous verses. Did some of his descendants or contemporaries, revolted by his bloodlust, also begin to worship the LORD? We are not told. If they did, they were pagans who became saints.

But should Genesis 4:26b be regarded in this way? Certainly the Divine Name is included in the Hebrew text of this verse. But what weight can be put on that? We have been taking it at face value and regarding it as declaring that the people referred to not only knew of the existence of the Name but actually used it in their invoking of God. Not only would the majority of non-evangelical Old Testament scholars disagree with this but even some evangelical ones as well, though not in exactly the same terms. They would all refuse to affirm that the patriarchs knew Elohim as Yahweh, pointing to Exodus 6 verses 2 and 3 as proof.

EXODUS 6:2 & 3

It might appear at first sight that a study of this verse belongs simply to the field of Old Testament scholarship and that it has no bearing what-soever on our subject. But that could not be further from the truth. A case could actually be made out for saying that one's view on this matter determines one's view on the question of the salvation of the unevangelised. To show that it is relevant requires a discussion which could be technical. We will try to simplify it because it is so relevant.

In the heyday of the Higher Criticism of the Pentateuch it was axiomatic to regard the statement in Exodus 6:2 and 3 as meaning that the Name was only made known at the time of Moses and in the Exodus. Consequently, all the references to Yahweh in Genesis were not authentic for the people and the periods referred to. This was the corner-stone of the old Documentary Hypothesis and of the evolutionary view of the development of the religion of Israel. Just as Genesis-Deuteronomy was the result of a combination of different sources over a period of time, so Old Testament religion was regarded as a compound of differing religious views and practices- some from the surrounding nations. Obviously this opens the door to a partial recognition of other gods and religions as being valid.

Alec Motyer responded to this in his monograph entitled 'The Revelation of the Divine Name'. Though published over thirty years ago, it was, along with the work of Professor W.J.Martin of Liverpool University, a landmark in evangelical study of the Pentateuch in the United Kingdom. Motyer and Martin dealt with the Documentary Hypothesis and defended the Mosaic authorship of the first five books of the Bible. Their work is by no means outdated.

After making due allowance for the fact that the biblical writer made references to Yahweh, Motyer showed that in at least 45 out of 116 occurrences, between Genesis 12:1 and Exodus 6:2 and 3, the term Yahweh was either used by the patriarchs of God, or by God himself. He then argued that the Hebrew terms in Exodus 6:2 and 3 did not mean that the Name was completely unknown but that its significance had not been previously disclosed. He presented and argued for the following translation of the verse: 'And God spoke to Moses, and said to him: I am Yahweh. And I showed myself to Abraham, to Isaac, and to Jacob in the character of El Shaddai, but in the character expressed by my name Yahweh I did not make myself known to them'. He argued that these verses did:

> 'not deny to the patriarchs the knowledge of the name
> Yahweh, but only (the) knowledge of the significance of
> the Name........These words tell us plainly that what
> Moses was sent to Egypt to declare was not a Name but a
> nature'.[11]

Certainly Motyer's line of exegesis is much better than the old liberal view which many Old Testament scholars are now seeking to move away from without actually declaring it to be wrong. To regard the

Name as being previously known certainly precludes the possibility of other gods and religions being approved of in the Old Testament record. But two questions remain unanswered. The first is what about the pre-Abrahamic period, that is Genesis 1-11? Did Noah, Enosh and Adam and Eve for example also know of the Name? Secondly, is it entirely satisfactory to say that though the Name was known, the nature which corresponded to it was not? We will return to these questions.

Contemporary evangelical Old Testament scholars, for example Gordon Wenham and Chris Wright, take a different line with reference to Exodus 6 and the previous uses of the Name. They do not pass over those uses in silence as Pinnock does. But what they do is to use the distinction between the final edition of the text and the time reference in the text to cast doubt on whether the patriarchs knew God as Yahweh. In the words of Wenham:

> *'Is this identification of the patriarchs' God with that of Moses a theological assertion by the writer of Genesis, who was sure the same God had spoken to Abraham as spoke to Moses? Or do the statements in Genesis implying that Yahweh revealed himself to the patriarchs correspond to the patriarchs' own conception of the God they worshipped?'.*[12]

The result of this distinction needs to be spelt out in order to be understood. Let us take an example. In Genesis 15:6 we read 'Abram believed the LORD and he credited it to him as righteousness'. Using the view that this statement is the author's (editor's) report means that Abram was, in terms of his knowledge, not believing in Yahweh but El or El Shaddai. But the (final) editor of the Genesis text knew that El was Yahweh and so what he wrote was true as a fact, but it was not true as a description of what had gone on in Abram's mind. Following that line of thinking would mean adopting the position that while it was Yahweh whom Abram knew, he did not know him as Yahweh.

As El was the chief god of the Canaanite pantheon, such a distinction as Wenham and Wright accept and employ opens the door to an endorsement of syncretism in the biblical narrative. Wright is aware of that possibility and therefore poses the following question:

> *'Are we then to regard the faith of Israel as syncretistic in its origins and early development, and if so, does this constitute biblical support for a syncretistic stance by the Christian vis-a-vis contemporary world faiths?'.*[13]

He answers this question by defining syncretism and differentiating it from 'accommodation or assimilation'. He writes:

> *'Syncretism is a conscious or unconscious attempt to combine divergent religious elements (beliefs, rites, vocabulary) in such a way that a new religious mixture evolves which goes beyond the contributing elements. It presupposes that none of the contributing elements can be regarded as final or sufficient in itself'.*

He continues:

> *'It must be distinguished from the modes by which God has communicated his self-revelation using existing concepts and religious forms, but then transcending and transforming them with a new theology. The latter process is usually called accommodation or assimilation. It is quite different from syncretism inasmuch as it recognizes the reality of unique divine revelation in history, whereas syncretism excludes such a category a priori'.*[14]

We would be happy to leave the matter there if that were the only 'danger' inherent in Wenham and Wright's position. This is because we also see in the Bible that God does condescend to make himself known in an alien context only to break that mould by subsequent disclosures. A wedge of grace creates a divide which opens into a chasm with every further divine disclosure.

But another question can be raised on the basis of the editor/patriarch distinction. Wright sees this and expresses the question as follows:

*'Can we infer from the Genesis story that men may
worship and relate personally to the true, living God but
under the name or names of some "local" deity and
without knowledge of God's saving name and action in
Christ?'* [15]

In answer to this important question Wright points out that God's self-disclosure to Abraham 'in terms of divine names' which he would have already known 'in no way implies that all Abraham's contemporaries who worshipped El in his various manifestations, and with the seamier side of his mythology, thereby knew and worshipped the living God'. Wright sees God's relationship with Abraham as being based on an act of divine grace and not on a disclosure of divine names.

So far, so good, we may think. The caveats which Wright introduces should prevent anyone from deducing that what is being claimed is that all gods are ultimately one and the same and that all religions are ways of salvation. He also denies that all will be saved. But there are two loopholes or possibilities which are left open by the denial that the divine Name was known prior to the Exodus.

Wenham points out the first which is that the pre-Mosaic era was much freer and more benign than the Sinaitic in terms of its view of other gods and religions. He writes as follows:

*'This distinction between the El revelation of Genesis and
the Yahweh revelation of later times is more than a verbal
contrast. The exclusiveness, holiness, and strictness of the
God of Exodus is absent from Genesis. Though the
patriarchs are faithful followers of their God, they enjoy
good relations with men of other faiths. There is an air of
ecumenical bonhomie about the patriarchal religion
which contrasts with the sectarian exclusivenesss of the
Mosaic age and later prophetic demands'.* [16]

Something is being felt for in this statement for which there is no evidence in Genesis. There is not a hint of patriarchal involvement with Canaanite religion in that book.

Secondly, to adopt the view that says that the patriarchs did not know the name Yahweh means that it becomes possible to argue that just as the patriarchs knew (the true) God savingly, without knowing the name Yahweh, so may others today, without knowing of the name of Jesus Christ. Wright concedes this possibility and includes in it those like Noah and Enosh, Adam and Eve, that is those who lived before Abraham. Here is the beginning of the contemporary divide among evangelicals between those who adopt only a christocentric view of the way of salvation and those who also take an epistemological view. The former see salvation as being only in Christ, but the latter see faith as also necessary.

But we are not prepared to accept this understanding of Exodus 6:2 and 3 and of the faith of the men and women who lived before Moses, including those who antedated the patriarchs. We do not think that Joshua 24:14 with its reference to the other gods which were served by the fathers of Israel before the era of bondage means that they served El not Yahweh. The statement can quite acceptably refer to the gods which were served prior to Abram's call. We submit these two reasons for this conclusion. First, it seems to us that Motyer has demonstrated that the Hebrew of Exodus 6:2 and 3 does not *demand* the view that the Name was unknown before Moses. Secondly, the uses of the Divine Name in Genesis 12-50 and in 1-11 (though Motyer does not mention those chapters) can be taken at their face value. As they are infrequent, they do not appear to be the result of reading back subsequently given revelation. If that was what the writer wanted to do surely he would have done it more often.

The view we therefore propose is as follows. We begin with Motyer's position that Exodus 6:2 and 3 refers to the disclosure of the meaning of the name rather than of the name itself. The name Yahweh was not unknown prior to Moses. Was his mother's name not Jochebed, which is a compound of an abbreviation of the name Yahweh?

Even so it was primarily as El or El Shaddai that the patriarchs knew God. That name came to the fore in their times because Jehovah wished to stress his ability to transform his people (the three patriarchs were named or re-named by El Shaddai) and to perform his promises alone.

El Shaddai means 'God Almighty' and points to divine omnipotence. It provides a rich background for the disclosure of what was implicit in the name Yahweh, the use of which consequently declined in that period.

However, we dare to wonder whether even Motyer overstates the contrast by using the name/nature distinction. Was it the case that prior to Moses and the Exodus *nothing* of God's nature was known which corresponded to the name Yahweh? Have we not seen that Adam, Eve, Enosh, Lamech, Noah and even Abraham knew something of that nature? Does not that evidence point to there being *some* connection in the minds of people between the Name and the promise of a coming deliverer? In turn, does this not indicate *some* knowledge of a 'saving God' existing and surviving to *some* degree within that line of descent marked by the names Adam, Abel, Seth, Enosh, Enoch, Noah, Shem and Abraham?

In one place in his monograph Motyer admits that something of the nature which corresponded to the Name was known to Abraham. In a remarkably powerful and spiritually perceptive piece of writing, he says:

> '*But, as so often in the Bible, the light which will shine in fullness only at some future date is too strong wholly to be restrained from earlier ages, and here and there breaks through in hints and suggestions which are only appreciated when at last the moment of unveiling comes. Once in Genesis such a beam of light fell. When Abraham, on the mountain, found that God had indeed provided a sacrifice, and when he offered the ram in manifest substitution for his son, then, for a brief second he caught and expressed the truth, "Yahweh sees, Yahweh provides". Here only is the divine name elaborated in pre-Mosaic religion, and Yahweh is declared to be the God who meets his people in their extremity, when the chosen seed is at the point of extinction, and Himself provides the redemption price'.*

But then Motyer goes further - and this is what we have been arguing for in claiming that Genesis 3:15 and the name provided in embryonic form all that would be subsequently unfolded in Scripture about salvation. Motyer writes movingly as well as brilliantly:

> *'The mountain top scene could hardly be expounded even in this detail except that the full light was later unveiled, and God showed His nature. The exodus is, on a large scale, what Mount Moriah is in miniature. The same God who provided the ram provided also the Passover Lamb. There is no further truth about God ever to be revealed; even we, who have been permitted to see the light of the knowledge of the glory of God in the face of Jesus Christ, see only the truth of the exodus - "his exodus which he would accomplish in Jerusalem" -and when, in God's mercy, we meet the Lord in the air, it will be to discover that once again God has done that which his name declares: He has gone down to Egypt to redeem His people: for this is His name for ever, and this is His memorial unto all generations'.*[17]

This background therefore accounts for the knowledge of the 'pagan saints' before and up to Noah and makes it impossible for them to be regarded as 'pagan' on Pinnock's definition of that word which was 'an outsider'. They were *insiders* in terms of the circle to whom revelation was vouchsafed. They were indeed saints.

All this casts an interesting and important light on our whole subject. As has been pointed out, it is certainly relevant as the informing context for the knowledge of so-called 'pagan saints' in the pre-diluvian period. But it is also to be remembered with reference to what followed after the Flood. Noah and Shem knew of the revelation, and Japheth too. It did not die out with the Flood. It would therefore have been transmitted to posterity, diminishing in some families as time passed because of the increasing effects of sin, but being augmented in others by the onward unfolding of special revelation. In those years up to the pre-Sinai era, to be outside the covenant line was not ipso facto to be destitute of *all* knowledge of Yahweh.

'PAGAN SAINTS' AFTER THE FLOOD

Having concluded that those pre-diluvians whom Pinnock describes as 'pagan saints' should not be so categorised because they were recipients of saving revelation, we move on to consider what he has to say about those who lived after the Flood. We have already mentioned one of these at the end of the previous chapter, namely Rahab. She was a pagan who became a saint. Another can be dealt with very quickly: Lot cannot be a 'pagan' saint either. He was a relative of Abram by marriage and, more importantly, he 'went with him'. He therefore comes within the circle of Pre-Israel, just as Abram did.

Two others stand out in Pinnock's book as being particularly important to his case. They are Melchizedek in the Old Testament and Cornelius in the New. We will give pride of place to these in our comment. But before doing that there are some others whom Pinnock mentions about whom something ought to be said. We will try to consider carefully all that is said in the Scriptures about these individuals.

Abimelech

There is an obvious similarity between the incident recorded here, or rather what occasioned it, and what is found in Genesis 12:10-20. In both, Sarai's beauty led Abram to fear that he would be put to death by those who found her attractive. This was not altogether groundless as both the Egyptian Pharaoh and the Philistine, Abimelech, did take her into their harems. But the real basis of Abram's concern was that he thought that he was among people who had no 'fear of God'. That is made explicit by his own admission which is recorded in Genesis 20:11.

Though it is Abimelech who exhibits the clearer evidence of a knowledge of God - and it is he whom Pinnock names and not Pharaoh - we ought not to overlook the fact that the latter expressed a real sense of moral indignation in his questioning of Abram. He knew that wrong had been done to him and that consequently he had been put in a false position. In addition, some calamity had fallen upon him and his household. Where had such knowledge come from? Pharaoh does not attribute it to any deity. However he came by the knowledge of what

Abram had done, the main aspects of his moral outlook are traceable to the fact that all men, by virtue of having been made in the image and likeness of God, have a knowledge of right and wrong and of the fact that the wrong merits punishment (Romans 2:14-16). A comparison can be made here with the thinking of the irreligious and uneducated natives of Malta (see Acts 28:4) who linked calamity with crime or sin.

Abimelech had a greater intimacy with and knowledge of God than Pharaoh. He received a communication from God and referred to God as sovereign. He too knew that sin merited punishment - and once again a punishment had fallen - but he also knew that God would not punish the innocent. How did he come by that degree of knowledge? Is it not compatible with what was revealed by creation and to Noah and his sons, for Abimelech was a descendant of Ham. We think it is.

Taking this view of Abimelech's knowledge does not mean that no room is left for the element of surprise, or the unexpected, which is necessary to Abram's part in the history. Abram was neither being proud nor disdainful in looking down on others who had 'no fear of God', a synonym for true religion. Having come from paganism in Ur, he knew that sin debased and corrupted. It was that, coupled with the weakness of his own faith, which lay behind his half truth, or his half lie.

But what of Abimelech's protestation that he had acted 'in the integrity of his heart' (Gen. 20:5)? Though this is acknowledged by God (verse 6), it is endorsed only as a fact and is not tantamount to a divine declaration that he was wholly sinless in the matter. All it means is that God knew that Abimelech genuinely did not know that Sarai was Abram's wife when he took her into his household. Pinnock tends to overdraw the contrast between his behaviour and that of Abram and greatly overstates the case when he describes Abimelech as a man of 'faith' and 'of complete integrity'.

As a matter of fact, Abimelech was told by God that he had been kept from committing the sin which he intended to perform in taking Sarai. Consequently, he needed to take divinely prescribed steps to avoid death. This is certainly not the depiction of one who is 'going to heaven' because of his 'faith'. Abimelech needed to make amends for his own misdemeanour, even though it was Abram who had sinned against him. When he did this, God, through Abram's intercession, removed the judgment which had been visited on the females in Abimelech's household. While Abimelech is described as calling God 'Lord' (Adhonai) that is ruler or master, it is God who is Yahweh who sends deliverance from judgments.

Jethro, Rahab, Ruth and Naaman

All these can be bracketed together because they end up acknowledging Yahweh. They therefore become saints indeed. But what were they before? Jethro or Reuel (Exodus 18) was Moses' father in law. He was also a priest in the land of Midian. We are not told of how he addressed the deity whom he served but the likelihood is that he had not recognised the 'LORD' though he knew of the designation 'God'. This can be seen by comparing verse 1 with verse 11. He comes to Moses because he had heard of all that 'God' had done for Israel and after being told by Moses (verse 8) of all that the LORD had done, he worships the LORD as greater than all the gods of the Egyptians. This is an account of someone becoming a saint and that is what the narrative emphasises - not his state prior to that. The very same thing has been shown to be the case with Rahab in the preceding chapter.

Similarly, the profession of faith which Ruth makes is a glorious example of a pagan coming to trust in Yahweh, the God of Israel (see Ruth 1:15-18). Unlike Orpah, Ruth left her own people land and gods and trusted in the protection of the wings of Yahweh (2:11 and 12). In her adoption of Naomi's God and people for her own, there is an echo of the covenant promise which is repeatedly extended to Israel by Yahweh -'I will be your God and you shall be my people'.

Naaman gives expression to a similar knowledge after he had been cleansed from leprosy. He acknowledges one God who is the LORD. (see II Kings 5:15-18) These were pagans who became saints. To speak of them as 'pagan saints' is to go against the purpose of the scriptural record which is to present their recognition of Yahweh.

Melchizedek

The case of Melchizedek (Genesis 14:18-24) is probably the strongest

Old Testament illustration of Pinnock's argument. This is because Melchizedek is described as 'a priest of El Elyon' which means 'God Most High' and as such superior to Abram in a religious sense.

Pinnock regards him as 'a believer outside the line of Abraham'. While that lineage is likely and we grant it, we are not convinced that he was not a Semite. Admittedly, we cannot prove that he was a descendant of Shem, though his name is Semitic. But Pinnock needs to prove that he was not a Semite in order to make his point, that he was a 'pagan' saint, stick. If he were a Semite, he was an insider, a recipient of saving revelation and a member of the chosen line. We think that he was.

We are not forgetting that his parentage was deliberately (divinely) screened from view in the Old Testament. That strange fact in a book which is full of genealogies is explained to us in the New Testament (see Hebrews 5-7). The reason for the omission was certainly not to support Pinnock's case that a priest of a heathen religion had a faith in God which was genuine! His interpretation of the whole incident reflects the axe which he is grinding. It is as follows:

> 'God was giving Abram a positive experience of the
> religious culture around him, to tell him not to be puffed
> up or feel superior ... as if his election (meant) the
> exclusive possession of God'.[18]

However, we recall that revelation had been given to and declared by Noah about Yahweh's saving purpose with reference to his sons (Genesis 9:24-7). That would have been known to them all and to some degree to their descendants. Given that background, can Melchizedek be regarded as a complete outsider?

This same reply can be made to Pinnock's description of Job as 'a pagan held up as a model of righteousness and piety in both Old and New Testaments..... a believer outside the line of Abraham'. It is by no means impossible that Job was a Semite: Uz was a descendant of Shem (cf.Gen. 10:22 and 23) and people often gave their names to cities and territories. In addition the name Yahweh is used once in the book of Job and it is on Job's own lips (12:9). On this understanding,

Job was not an outsider (pagan), either.

But to revert to Melchizedek, if we set aside the position that he was a 'pagan' priest, then all the facts which are recorded in Genesis 14, which Pinnock lists in support of his own viewpoint, appear in a very different light. We will summarise them with regard to Melchizedek and Abram.

It is true that Melchizedek did declare himself to be a priest of 'El Elyon - God Most High'. But this does not have to be a deity other than the One whom Abram knew and worshipped. Melchizedek was a representative of the older religion which was fashioned in response to God's self-revelation in Creation, Fall and Flood, but from which all reference to Yahweh and the significance of the Name had dropped out. Therefore, to draw an implied parallel between his religion and Hinduism or Buddhism is not to compare like with like at all.

It is also true that Abram did respond to Melchizedek in ways which were incontestably religious. But that does not mean, as Pinnock asserts, that he was 'accepting the equivalence of Yahweh and El Elyon and the validity of Melchizedek's worship'. When Abram received a blessing and gave tithes, he did both in the name of '*Yahweh* El Elyon'. What does this combination of the name of Melchizedek's god with the name of Yahweh mean? It cannot mean that Abram was opposing Yahweh and El Elyon. Does it mean only that he was equating them? Surely it means that he was supplementing the inadequate knowledge which Melchizedek possessed with the revelation which he himself had been given. The Creator of heaven and earth was in reality Yahweh, the deliverer. There is no word about Abram's crediting *Melchizedek's* religion or his worship. Abram was consciously worshipping Yahweh in submitting to Melchizedek's ministrations.

Pinnock regards the meeting with Melchizedek as calculated to humble Abram but another view of the whole incident has at least an equal claim to be considered in the light of Genesis 14:1-16 and 15:1. Indeed, it has more going for it when considered in the light of the use of this passage in the Epistle to the Hebrews. It is that God brought Melchizedek to meet Abram not in order that he might be humbled but that he might be strengthened. The strengthening of believers was the pastoral purpose of the writer to the Hebrews in introducing the Melchizedek typology in Hebrews 5:10 and 6:20. We will present this alternative interpretation with respect to Genesis 14 and 15.

The four kings whom Abram pursued had only been routed, losing all their possessions and captives. On returning from this successful expedition, Abram was first met by the king of Sodom whose people he had recovered in the course of seeking to deliver Lot, his own nephew. Then the king of Salem appeared. How is Abram, the victor, going to deal with these two kings? It will be in the light of what they say to him and how it relates to the revelation which he has already been given.

The king of Salem speaks of God Most High and the blessing which he had already given Abram in routing the kings. Abram, the believer in God who is Yahweh, understands that language and responds positively. The same God is speaking to him, who has spoken to him before. But the king of Sodom speaks abruptly, offering earthly goods as a return for services rendered. Abram sees that as a temptation to turn from God the LORD, and sets it aside.

He has thus given away all he has gained. What he has given to Melchizedek is given as a token of thanks and faith in Yahweh, God most high. The rest, apart from what was due to his retinue, is given to the king of Sodom as being of no worth to one who had all necessary things in God the LORD. Ignoring the chapter division, he is then given an assurance from Yahweh that he will be defended and rewarded. Defence was needed because the routed kings could return to wreak their revenge. Recompense was appropriate because of all that he had parted with.

This passage is therefore about the uniqueness of Yahweh who is the Most High and about the sufficiency of faith in him alone. Melchizedek is thus an authentic type of the Lord Jesus Christ whose regal high-priestly ministry defends and enriches his believing people.

Endnotes

1. Pinnock op.cit.

2. ibid.p.101

3. ibid.p.101

4. ibid.p.101

5. ibid.p.107

6. ibid.p.92

7. ibid.p.105

8. ibid.p.21

9. ibid.p.21

10. ibid p.24

11. Motyer op.cit. pp.11 & 16

12. The religion of the patriarchs in Essays on the Patriarchal Narratives. eds A.R.Millard & D.J.Wiseman IVP 1980 pp.157,8

13. The christian and other religions: the biblical evidence. C.J.H.Wright. Themelios January 1984 P.6.

14. ibid.p.6

15. ibid.p.6

16. Wenham op.cit p.184

17. Motyer op.cit.p 30

18. Pinnock op.cit. p.94

Pagan Saints! — In the New Testament

There are several individuals who are mentioned in the pages of the New Testament whom Pinnock lists as coming into the category of 'pagan saints'. In the Gospels there are the Magi, two centurions and the Syro-Phoenician woman. They all originated from outside the borders of Palestine and were not members of the covenant community. Yet they seem to have been expressing faith. In the book of Acts there is the notable, and possibly crucial, example of Cornelius. We will consider each of these, giving most of our attention to the latter.

The Magi (Matthew 2:1-12)

There are many questions which are raised by this remarkable piece of history. Though Matthew records that these men came from the East, he is not more specific as to their homeland. Discussion continues on that point with Persia and Babylon being the strongest possibilities. Similarly, the exact meaning of "magoi", the term used by Matthew, is debated. Does it have a racial as well as a professional dimension to its meaning? If it is only the latter, which profession is in view? We adopt the view which many hold that they were astrologers. Happily, we need not go further into a discussion of these matters because all that is required for our purpose is that it be accepted that these men were not from Palestine and were not members of the covenant community. They were outsiders, that is 'pagans' in Pinnock's sense of the term.

The material point is that they had recognised a particular star as having a special significance. It indicated that the king of the Jews had been born and they had followed it with the intention of paying him the homage due to a king.

What does this tell us about the source of their knowledge? Sadly, not very much, either in terms of how they came by it or how they were able to deduce the significance of the star as they did. But it is not vital to establish that either, in order to consider them from the perspective of 'pagan saints'. What is all important about these men is that they intended to *worship* the King of the Jews. Even though this may not amount to a recognition of his deity and probably does not, it does point to his messiahship. The fact that they are intent on submitting to the kingship of Jesus, though an infant, is a fact of no mean significance. This tells us that they were pagans who became saints.

But Pinnock offers the following explanation of their quest:

> 'something in their religious culture must have pointed them to Palestine making them want to seek the coming one and open their treasures to him'.[1]

We would be happy to accept this as a suggestion if the expression 'their religious culture' did not carry the freight which Pinnock loads it with. He means that they sought the King of the Jews because of what they learned from *any source except saving revelation* and that they were accepted by God *before* they came to Jesus. It is true that they could have come, drawn by anything, we know not what or how, and finding Jesus, worship him as the promised Messiah. That can happen in a world in which God is sovereign and works mysteriously. The only problem, however, in accepting this scenario lies in saying that in effect they did not need to come to be saved.

But there is one other way of regarding these men which advances an explanation of how they came by the knowledge which they possessed. It is only a theory but we mention it because it is not without supporting evidence and it has not been shown to be impossible. In the book of Daniel which is set in Babylon there are references to magicians. These are not to be thought of as conjurers or worse. It is true that some were charlatans (cf. Acts 8:9; 13:6,8). But others were seekers after truth by whatever means they could find. Some studied dreams; others the stars;

and some read books, especially those which claimed to have something about the future.

There was a large Jewish community in Babylon whose history stretched back to the days of the sixth century. Daniel himself had been influential among the wise men of Babylon, as is indicated in the Old Testament book which bears his name. We also know that the study of earlier Old Testament records was a feature of that time (Daniel 9:2). There is a prediction in Numbers 24:17 which reads 'A star will come out of Jacob; a sceptre will rise out of Israel'. This was declared by Balaam who himself came from the East (Numbers 23:7) and it was widely regarded among the Jews as a messianic prophecy. Assuming that such a statement was accessible in Babylon to any who wished to search it out and that it was understood that a star would appear to herald the birth of that victorious king, we are provided with an explanation of the believing knowledge of the Magi. But that would make them believers and not 'pagans' because they had some saving revelation.

Either way then, the Magi could not have been 'pagan saints'. They were either 'pagans' who did become saints by coming to Jesus, which means that they were not saints before, or they were saints before and therefore could not have been 'pagans'.

The Centurions (Matthew 8:10; 27:54; Mark:15:39; Luke 7:9; 23:47)

These references relate to two different Roman soldiers in charge of a hundred men; the first two to an incident in the life and ministry of Jesus while the last three are related to his crucifixion. The Lord commends the first centurion for his faith; the second, by the very nature of the situation only has his testimony recorded, but we may deduce that it is commended as genuine. It is the first who is really relevant to this investigation but the second is surely an example of a pagan who became a saint.

With regard to the first, it is clear that he had faith. The Lord not only draws attention to it but describes it as 'such faith'. There was therefore something surprising and distinctive about it. The Lord not only responded to it by granting his request but also by making him an object lesson to those around. What was special about it? It was that he perceived the nature of Jesus' authority. It was like his own. It was delegated from one greater and it was instantaneously effective. He thus perceived the very nature of the messiahship of Jesus as being by divine appointment and divine empowering. In addition, he rejected any notion of his own personal worth, contradicting the Jews' commendation of him to Jesus.

Both these men came to a believing recognition of Jesus as the Christ. Their faith was in him as Lord and one of them was commended for that by the Lord. They are therefore analogous to those in the Old Testament who came to acknowledge God as Yahweh. They were pagans who became saints.

The Syro-Phoenician woman (Matthew 15: 22)

What has been said about the centurions can be said of this descendant of Israel's age old enemies. She left her native territory and began to call loudly after Jesus in spite of the great displeasure which the disciples expressed and the stony silence which Jesus maintained. Even when Jesus explained his dismissive treatment of her to his disciples, she did not give up. She eventually confronted him only to be told that she was an outsider not only as far as the Jews were concerned but as far as Jesus was concerned. Knowing what he was doing, he used the Jewish term of opprobrium for her, saying that dogs were not given the food which belonged to children. Even that did not silence her because having by implication been called a dog (an 'unclean' Gentile), she counters by saying that there are usually some crumbs for little dogs which the children do not miss.

She is justly commended, not for her skill at repartee, but for her great faith. She had come to Jesus as the 'Son of David'. She believed in him as the promised Messiah even though she was an outsider. Though we are not told how she came to believe this, we are told that it was because of her need and her knowledge of him that she came and did not give up. She was a pagan who had become a saint.

Cornelius (Acts 10:1-11:18)

Pinnock refers to this narrative as 'the most influential story of this sort in Scripture', by which he means that Cornelius constitutes the clearest example in the Bible of a 'pagan saint'. We are ready to acknowledge that if Pinnock's exegesis of this passage stands, then his general case is substantiated. We therefore proceed to examine the all important statement in this passage which is in Acts 10:34 and 35. It reads :'I now realise how true it is that God does not show favouritism but accepts men from every nation who fear him and do what is right'.

It will be seen from looking at these words of Peter in their actual setting in the passage, that they say something about Cornelius before Peter preached the gospel to him. But their scope of reference is universal. Everyone, everywhere who resembles Cornelius in faith and conduct is also accepted by God. This is therefore a very important statement. Pinnock's comment on it is as follows:

> 'Before he heard the gospel, Cornelius was a God-fearing
> believer. He was a Gentile in a good and acceptable rela-
> tionship with God ... one of those men of faith outside the
> covenant communities of Judaism and Christianity. God
> was present with him in the religious sphere of his pagan
> life. Peter is saying that those like Cornelius who have
> faith in God, wherever they may live in the whole world,
> are accepted by God in the way Abraham was accepted,
> on the basis of faith'.[2]

It will be remembered that we have readily acknowledged the fact that God does work directly in the wider world that is without the instrumentality of the church's witness (see one interpretation of the Magi). To deny that he does that and to try to explain the 'faith' of Cornelius before Peter visited him would be a difficult task indeed. But our position does not impose that constraint on us. Not only so, we are even ready to go further in seeking to come to terms with Cornelius prior to Peter's visit. We can say that God, in leading someone to himself, might use the attractions of another religion to produce changes in behaviour patterns in people's lives. God can work from within any religion or none. To admit that presents no difficulty because Paul teaches that Christians are to provoke Jews to envy by their exhibition of the glories of God's grace through their fellowship with Jesus Christ (Romans 11:11). The hearts of all are open to the Lord and he can use the most unexpected thing to work in them.

Cornelius is a case in point of this very thing. He was a Gentile who became a God-fearer and in all probability that was as the result of the influence of Judaism presenting a sharp contrast with the philosophy and mythology of polytheism which had governed him before. Though he was not circumcised, he attended the synagogue, prayed to the God of the Jews and gave alms.

Even though we admit this, the difficulty which we have with Pinnock's statement is that he equates Cornelius with Abraham in terms of faith and acceptance with God, and that prior to Peter's visit and his hearing the gospel through him. We must first inquire into the basis on which he does this and secondly into how he understands what happened to Cornelius as a result of Peter's visit. This means investigating what is meant in these chapters by the term 'accepted' in 10:35 and 'saved' in 11:14.

WHAT DOES 'ACCEPTED' MEAN?

It is perhaps significant that Luke does not use the term 'faith' when referring to Cornelius. This means at least that great care should be taken by anyone who desires to use it in a discussion of this narrative. We are ready not to oppose its use provided more is not included in it than is actually warranted at any given point by the text.

The opening verses of chapter 10 declare Cornelius to be 'devout' and describe his piety in relation to his household, the Jewish people and the Jewish religion. He gave alms and engaged in prayer at the set times of day. He was a God-fearer. He had not actually become a proselyte but he attended the synagogue. He was therefore not a member of the Jewish community. On this reading, he was a 'pagan', an outsider.

In that condition, an angel of God appears to him in a vision. He declares that God has taken note of his worship in exactly the same way as of sacrifices duly and sincerely offered. That is indicated by the word 'memorial' which in the Old Testament describes the acceptability of true sacrifice to God. (Leviticus 2:2,9,16) It is to that spiritual condition that the word 'accepted' in verse 35 relates. Further, it is illustrated by the vision which was given to Peter demonstrating that what was previously regarded as unclean is so no longer. But this acceptance is not equivalent to salvation. That is shown by the fact that the angel of God directs Cornelius to send for Simon Peter so that he might hear more than he then knew and so be saved (see 10:22b,33; and 11:13 and 14).

The main question is whether the 'faith' of Cornelius *at this stage* of his experience, corresponds exactly to that of Abram. Pinnock says it does, but we disagree. The reason why we do so is that the faith of Abram is not merely a subjective faith, that is the grace of faith in the human heart. That faith is impossible to identify apart from its effects. Abram believed in something, or someone. His faith had an object, the LORD, and as yet he was not the object of Cornelius' devotion.

In the first use of the verb 'believe' in the book of Genesis (15:6), it was Yahweh who Abram believed in and in addition, it was the promise of a seed which was the specific object of his faith at this time. We have considered at length the use of the divine Name in Genesis and we want to argue that to regard this as meaning that Abram believed in El is inadequate in the light of the context. What did El say? He promised Abram 'a seed' in whom 'all the nations of the earth would be blessed'. To empty Abram's faith of a 'Yahweh-shaped' content is not adequate. Of course the substance corresponding to that shape was revealed in the Exodus, but there was something of it before. In Genesis 15:17 and 18 we have a covenant making ceremony in which Yahweh took the leading, the only part.

WHAT DOES 'SAVED' MEAN?

What has been said therefore about the meaning of the name Yahweh and its relationship with the first promise of a Messiah in Genesis 3:15 and the authenticity of its use by the patriarchs is relevant here.

Cornelius was relating to God; Abram to the God who was Yahweh who had promised a deliverer. In God's estimate, Cornelius needed to hear that his promise had been fulfilled in Jesus Christ so that his sins might be forgiven (Acts 10:43). The conclusion we therefore draw is that a parallel cannot be drawn between the 'faith' of Cornelius before Peter preached the gospel to him and that of Abram. At that time Cornelius was *not saved*.

Pinnock cannot accept this view because he regards Cornelius as already being fully accepted by God. The question therefore arises as to how he can explain the reference to salvation in 11:14. He does so by drawing a distinction between being accepted by God and becoming a Christian. He says that it was through hearing the gospel that Cornelius became a Christian but that does not mean that he was not accepted by God before. Bruce and Marshall do not take this view of 'accepted' in their comments on this passage.

Objecting to the view which necessitates the intervention of a human messenger to bring people to salvation, Pinnock argues:

> '*It ... implies that Cornelius was not already in a right rela-tionship with God before becoming a Christian. This means that Cornelius needed Peter in order to be saved from God's wrath. But this is not true. As Job in the Old Testament story, Cornelius did not need a special messenger to make him a believer. He was a believer already and not hellbound. True he needed to become a believer in order to receive messianic salvation, including assurance and the Holy Spirit, but not to be saved from hell*'. [3]

There is another way of understanding this Acts passage. It regards Cornelius as a 'believer' before Peter came to him but not on the grounds which Pinnock argues. In what he writes about Cornelius, he makes no reference to, or allowance for, the influence of the word of God which Cornelius would have heard read sabbath after sabbath, from the law and the prophets, in the synagogue. Given this word, it is therefore possible that Cornelius was a saint and not a 'pagan', an outsider, because even though he had not become a full Jew, he had saving revelation. Calvin comments on Acts 10:4 by saying:

'Whosoever came at that time into Judea he was enforced to hear somewhat of the Messiah, yea, there was some fame of him spread through countries which were far off. Wherefore, Cornelius must be put in the catalogue of the old fathers who hoped for salvation of the Redeemer before he was revealed'.[4]

However, we still feel that it is better not to take this line. If we adopt it we are brought into conflict with other statements in these chapters. We think that the conclusion of the apostles and the leaders of the church in Jerusalem expressed in 11:18 makes the view that Cornelius was saved before he heard the gospel impossible. There we read that Peter's rehearsal of what had happened in the house of Cornelius led them (Jewish believers) to conclude that God had granted to the Gentiles 'repentance unto life'. This means that prior to Peter's preaching and the effects associated with it, Cornelius and his household had not repented and had not received spiritual life. Therefore, not only were they not Christians but they were neither forgiven (10:43) nor renewed (10:45). In spite of every appearance to the contrary they were at that time liable to God's wrath.

We have sought to do justice to Pinnock's presentation on this point because of its importance to the overall case for the salvation of the heathen. If the Bible actually teaches that there were people who, without any knowledge of Yahweh, or of the coming Messiah or of the Lord Jesus Christ, were regarded by God as belonging to him and possessing eternal life, then the overall case is proved. The list of men and women of faith in Hebrews 11 does not do this either. It is intended to stress what faith enabled people to do rather than what it was they believed. Even so there are references to God's word, his promise and even to the Messiah (verses 3, 9 and 26) in the catalogue. It is therefore our view Pinnock has not succeeded in establishing his case.

'Pagan saints' is not just a striking epithet; it is a contradiction in terms, even in the sense in which Pinnock uses it. If those he refers to were 'pagans', that is total outsiders to saving revelation, then the Bible records that they actually became saints. If they had some saving revelation then they were insiders, saints indeed, and could not be 'pagans'.

ADDENDUM - POST-MORTEM SALVATION

The arguments which Pinnock and Cotterell advance for the salvation of the heathen as expressed in the titles of the last two chapters leave a lot to be desired. In our view, no one should feel under any pressure to accept them. There is, however, one further matter that Pinnock presents which must be considered. It is what he calls 'a post-mortem encounter with Christ' which would be saving. Carl Henry writes on this subject:

> *'The further notion of a decision for Christ even after death has been championed by modern Protestants troubled over the fate of multitudes who have never heard the gospel, and by missionary converts troubled over the tremendous infant mortality in some lands and/or over the fate of their own ancestors'.*[5]

Pinnock explores this subject in two ways in a chapter of his book entitled 'Hope for the Unevangelized'. He attempts to establish that the gospel will somehow be preached to people after their deaths and then considers who among them can be expected to believe in Christ and why. He is not arguing for universal salvation.

One of his sentences can be regarded as summing up the foundation for his case. He writes:

> *'Although the scriptural evidence for post-mortem encounter is not abundant, its scantiness is relativized by the strength of the theological argument for it'.*[6]

For Pinnock to say that evidence for this idea is 'not abundant' is indeed an understatement as there are only two passages in the Bible to which he can refer. Those passages are 1 Peter 3:19,20 and 4:6 and we must consider them. But first notice what Pinnock is really doing in the above statement. He is claiming theological credibility for something which lacks a firm exegetical base in the Scripture text. It is rather like the repeated (hopefully mythical!) story of a preacher's sermon notes left in the pulpit and seen by the caretaker who notices alongside one passage the written advice 'Argument weak. Shout here!'

In order to provide some semblance of an exegetical foundation for this view, Pinnock has to do two things. First of all he has to deal with Hebrews 9:27, a verse which quite clearly excludes what he is advancing and which has been understood throughout the history of the church as doing so. Secondly, he has to show that 1 Peter 3:19, 20 and 4:6 can support his view. We consider each.

Hebrews 9:27 declares 'Just as man is destined to die once and after this to face judgment'. In other words, death is the prelude to judgment. Pinnock's way of evading the plain sense of this text is not exegetical. He proceeds on the basis of assuming a post-mortem encounter and the opportunity to repent, which is what he has to prove. He calls theological considerations to his aid and uses the two facts that God does not cease to love sinners and that the judge is none other than the Saviour. He therefore reckons that there is no reason why mercy may not be sought and granted after death. His only uncertainty is whether those who have refused to seek it throughout their lives on earth, would do so then. Of course, his 'pagan saints' like Job would and others might too, though some, such as Herod or Hitler would not do so. He says categorically:

> 'The **opportunity** would be there for all to repent after death, but not necessarily the desire ' (emphasis original).[7]

But in saying all this, it is clear that he has side-stepped the plain meaning and force of Hebrews 9:27. There is no real place in his scheme of things for people being excluded from the bliss of heaven by the Lord Jesus Christ in just judgment, only that they exclude themselves through impenitence.

Secondly, does either passage in 1 Peter teach that *the gospel* will be preached to people *after* they have died? We take these verses in turn.

Does 1 Peter 3:19,20 refer to a preaching of the gospel to deceased people? The answer is no. Setting aside the possibility that it is Noah's preaching to his contemporaries by the Spirit which is being referred to in these verses, we note that the verb which Peter uses in 3:19 only means to make an announcement - the content and character of which is not indicated. It points to the act of a herald who may bring bad news as well as good. Taking the view that 'the spirits in prison' refer to evil spirits the verse yields the meaning that Christ proclaimed his triumph to them, sealing their doom.

In 1 Peter 4:6 the verb is different and does denote the proclamation of good news. But who are 'the dead' in this verse? Unlike 'the spirits' in 3:20, these are human beings. But in what sense are they dead? There are two possibilities. The first is that they were spiritually dead but physically alive. This would mean that through hearing the gospel preached, they would be made aware of God's displeasure against them in advance of the day of judgment, die to their own merit, believe the gospel and live to God. The other view understands the terms as referring to those who had died before the epistle was written but who, in their lifetimes, had heard the gospel preached to them.

Pinnock also includes the case of children as part of his argument. He writes:

> 'Scripture does not require us to hold that the window of opportunity is slammed shut at death. The fate of some may be sealed at death; those for example, who heard the gospel and declined the offer of salvation. But the fate of others is not sealed; babies, for example, who die in infancy. No one holds that death is the end of opportunity for them. The question is, would those who were capable of deciding for God in their lifetimes qualify for special treatment?'.[8]

The case of infants will be considered at the end of the next chapter but we do not think that Pinnock has correctly understood the case which has been presented for their salvation. In so far as the writer is aware, it is not grounded by anyone on a hearing of the gospel after death.

It therefore looks as if Pinnock has no foundation for his case in these verses and none available from any others. In our view that makes all his theologising superfluous. Not only has he to turn up the volume for his interpretation of the 1 Peter texts, he has to turn it down on Hebrews 9:27 which records that judgment comes after the appointment which all human beings have with death. Pinnock is avoiding the plain meaning of one text that is Hebrews 9:27 and trying to conjure up something out of another. This is much more like special pleading than sober exegesis. What contradicts his view is not heeded and what will not support his view is maintained.

The effect of all this is that the seriousness of the present in the light of eternity is being lost sight of. Carl Henry has posted a warning on this as follows:

> 'Some evangelical dissidents have challenged the scriptural emphasis that the spiritual decisions made in this life irrevocably determine human destiny (Hebrews 9:27). Some appeal to Revelation 21:25 (heaven's gates for ever open?) and to 1 Corinthians 15:29 (the enigmatic practice of baptism for the dead). Others appeal to Christ's preaching to imprisoned spirits (the dead?) in 1 Peter 3:19 and such declarations as that "every knee shall bow" (Philippians 2:10-11) and that God will be "all in all" (1 Corinthians 15:28)
>
> But is this a proper reading of texts in a narrative that everywhere stresses the need of immediate decision for Christ? And does not the theme "eat, drink and be merry for we can always nullify eternal consequences" dissolve the urgency of evangelism?'[9]

Endnotes

1. ibid.p.95

2. ibid. p.95

3. ibid p.167

4. Commentary on Acts Vol 1 p.414

5. Henry op.cit.

6. Pinnock op. cit. p.169

7. ibid pp.170,71

8. ibid.p.171

9. Henry op.cit.

Room for optimism

So far we have been considering *specific* arguments which have been advanced by evangelical and other scholars for the position that the unevangelised will be saved. For reasons which have been given, we have not found that any of these commands acceptance.

We are therefore still endorsing the view with which we began that it is necessary for everyone to believe in the Lord Jesus Christ in order to be saved and that means having to hear something about him. If there were no more to consider from the opposite side, our study could conclude at this point and the 'exclusivist' case could claim to be established. All that would be left to do would be to carry belief into practice and so to go into all the world with the gospel.

But, there is more to consider. To examine the stated arguments on the point of issue is not enough. The title of this chapter indicates that there is also now something of a mood or an attitude, something akin to the indefinable 'larger hope' of the liberals at the turn of the century. The very use of the term 'optimism' indicates that it is not only hard data and logical argument which enter into the reckoning: attitudes or (pre-) dispositions figure as well.

In the settling of doctrinal questions and disagreements, it is of course biblical exegesis and theological argument which are to be given pride of place. Even so, we think that it would be naive of anyone to imagine that it is only intellectual factors which are at work in such debates or discussions. Probably the dominant factor with regard to theological study today, in all its disciplines, is the recognition that as the student or interpreter comes to the text, he or she is already conditioned by all sorts of influences and not only theological ones.

In saying this, we are not suggesting that the differing positions adopted are *entirely* due to subjective motivations, nor that a dispute can be resolved *just* by the adoption and cultivation of other attitudes.

What is more, we freely recognise that we ourselves are part of this very scenario which we are describing. The subject matter of this inquiry creates emotional waves on both sides of the ship and that affects judgment, however hard one may strive to be fair and accurate.

To illustrate this, we are more than ready to admit that defenders of exclusivism have been among the chief detractors of the position which they uphold. In an address which Cotterell gave at the 1989 Evangelical Missionary Alliance conference, which was circulated in taped form, he recounted an incident which reinforces this very point. At a student meeting, he heard a speaker declare that all who did not believe in Jesus Christ would go to hell and that that was something about which he (the speaker) was glad. We find it as difficult to conceive of anyone saying that as to imagine that anyone who heard it would not be spiritually outraged. Cotterell heard the statement and experienced the reaction. We neither attribute his position to that experience nor exclude it from his thinking.

In the article entitled 'Evangelicals and Pluralism', to which reference has already been made, Gary Phillips helpfully and accurately divides evangelicals into exclusivists and inclusivists describing them as follows:

> 'Historically, evangelical exclusivists insist that Jesus
> Christ is necessarily both the **ontological** and the **episte-**
> **mological** basis of salvation. Those who die without
> placing faith in Christ in this life fall under condemnation.
> While evangelical inclusivists also affirm that Jesus Christ
> is the **ontological** basis of salvation, they insist that he
> need not be the **epistemological** basis' (emphasis original).

After making this clarifying statement with which we are in agreement, Phillips goes on to say correctly:

> 'There are still other positions which confuse these neat
> categories and therefore perplex many Christians'.[1]

These positions he describes as 'shades of agnosticism', identifying three kinds of evangelical agnostics. There are those who are neutral, those who are negative and those who are positive with regard to the subject. This way of speaking is not only an indication that our study has not been completed but that the way ahead is rather complicated. Agnosticism, we know, is a state of uncertainty, but talk of 'shades of agnosticism' leads to low visibility!

While we would not want to deny that there are shades of thought, as distinct from schools of thought among evangelicals on this matter, we do not find Phillips' categorisation of the neutral, the negative and the positive, as helpful as his previous statement about exclusivists and inclusivists. We prefer to use the term 'optimistic' or not, as the case may be. Our reasons are as follows.

First, Phillips places every evangelical in the agnostic category. Though he offers a particular reason for doing that which we will discuss, we do not think it helpful to describe as agnostic those who would deny that they are at all uncertain. Whether they are correct on the point or not is another matter, but at least they have the right to expect to be fairly represented. In addition a 'negative agnostic' is a difficult colour to work with indeed. Introducing the word 'optimistic' for others enables the exclusivist to be placed in the distinct category which his position requires because, examining the Bible, he sees no reason at all for believing that God will save the heathen without faith in Christ.

But secondly, Phillips has to admit in footnotes that two evangelicals, John Stott, who he places in the neutral agnostic category and Clark Pinnock, who is assigned to the positive agnostic category, no longer fit there. It would surely be better to drop the 'agnostic' tag altogether and adopt the term 'optimistic' as a category term for all who are neither negative nor neutral on this matter, using qualifying words like 'strongly' or 'mildly' to differentiate them further where necessary.

In this chapter, we will consider three positions taken by influential English non-exclusivists, moving through the range of response which is covered by the term 'optimism'. The first is an expression of strong optimism; the second, of neutrality, and the third, one of mild optimism, though its exponent actually prefers to be regarded as agnostic on the question. We will then refer to a piece of writing on our subject which has perhaps influenced the evangelical scene in the United States and in the United Kingdom more than all the explicitly theological writings put together. Finally, we will conclude with an examination of what is relevant to our inquiry in the Confessions of Faith produced in England in the seventeenth century.

BEING STRONGLY OPTIMISTIC

We consider under this heading the views of Sir Norman Anderson. For over twenty five years he presented a case which is, in essence, every bit as optimistic as that advanced by Cotterell and Pinnock, and which may, because they both quote him with respect, have even been formative of theirs. Some may be hesitant about his being bracketed along with these writers because his presentation of the case for the salvation of the unevangelised seems much less crusading and strident than theirs. But we think that this difference is due more to temperament and training than to lack of strong conviction on his part because, as has been mentioned, he argued his case on many occasions and over a considerable period of time. It is worth recording that Anderson put in print the following personal declaration which sounds every bit as definite as Cotterell is, or even Pinnock.

> '*I myself cannot doubt that there may be those who, while never hearing the gospel on earth, will wake up, as it were, on the other side of the grave to worship the One in whom, without understanding it at the time, they found the mercy of God*'.[2]

We proceed to review the case which Anderson presents. He begins from the firm base that the 'necessary and inescapable import' of John 14:6 and Acts 4:12 is that

> '*it is **only** through Christ that any man can come to a personal knowledge of (and fellowship with) God, and **only** through his life, death and resurrection that any man can come to an experience of salvation*'. (emphasis original).[3]

Consequently, he has to face the question of how that can apply to those in the Old Testament who lived before the coming of Christ.

He says that Abraham, Moses and David could be said to have come to know God through the Messiah whose coming they discerned to some degree. But what about all:

'the multitude of repentant and believing Jews who can scarcely be thought to have had any such vivid spiritual perception of what God was going to do in the future?'.[4]

His answer to the question of how these were accepted is that it was on the basis of Christ's death which was foreshadowed in the sacrifices which they brought and not on the basis of the sacrifices themselves. But while it is true that the virtue of the death of Christ was transmitted by God before its occurrence in time, it is far better and surely not impossible to regard the faith of all believing Jews in the Old Testament period as having been informed by what Abraham taught and what Moses and David wrote. There is therefore no need up to this point in Anderson's presentation to think of any one being accepted before God without faith in a promise or word regarding a coming Saviour. His argument can be stopped there.

Anderson, however, goes on to extend this principle of knowledge of God through faith, though not faith in a promised Christ, to people mentioned in the Bible who lived before Abraham and did not belong to Israel. (We have seen that there is biblical evidence that they had some word of promise too). But pursuing his line of exploration he takes the major step of including in his thinking 'those today who never heard the gospel', that is the 'countless millions'. The question which he poses is:

'Is there any basis on which the efficacy of the one atonement can avail those who have never heard about it?'[5]

To provide a solution to this awkward question, he knows that he cannot allow any diminution of the person and work of the Lord Jesus Christ. For him, the death of Christ is as much the only way to God for those who have heard the gospel as for those who have not heard it. What line can he explore for an answer?

He turns to the Old Testament saints for 'a ray of light' on the problem. He refers to their repentance and faith, the result of God's work in their hearts, as the means through which God's grace and mercy reached them on the basis of Christ's death. He then goes on to say two things, the second of which is often quoted but not the first. We will set both of them out as he presents them. They are:

> 'It is true that they had a special divine revelation in which to put their trust. But might it not be true of the follower of some other religion that the God of all mercy had worked in his heart by his Spirit, bringing him in some measure to realize his sin and need for forgiveness, and enabling him, in the twilight as it were, to throw himself on God's mercy?'[6]

We wish to point out that the first sentence does not provide a biblical basis for the hope tentatively expressed in the second. In fact, what it records is a reason for not expecting the event envisaged in the second to occur. Anderson acknowledges the fact of the promise made known as the precise difference between the Old Testament saints and the unevangelised, but then ignores it.

The Old Testament saints had a word about salvation and that made, and makes, all the difference. That God often has begun to work by his Spirit without the word is one thing, and we rejoice in such sovereign activity; that he accepts someone who believes without the word of promise is another. Surely if he can work directly by his Spirit in dead hearts, may he not be expected to guide his servants, even disobedient ones like Jonah, or reluctant ones like Peter, to take the gospel to such? Anderson's use of the Cornelius incident tries to disconnect what God has so clearly joined together in that passage: the seeking for God and the hearing of the gospel.

The Evangelical Alliance (U.K.) has published a statement, drawn up by one of its working groups, on the subject of Christianity and other Faiths and in it the question of the salvation of the unevangelised is dealt with. In its interaction with Scripture it covers much the same ground and uses the same arguments as Pinnock and Cotterell and so we will not repeat them. We mention this report under this heading because of the way in which it shows high regard for the comments of Sir Norman Anderson and agrees with his position. We will quote its final paragraph:

> *'salvation is indeed through Christ alone, won for humanity through "the one full, perfect and sufficient sacrifice for the sins of the whole world" which he offered upon the Cross; but this does not necessarily mean that it is limited to those who hear, understand and consciously respond in a positive way to his message. There are those too who, like Cornelius, have a sense of loving dependence upon God and a hope in his mercy without ever having heard that message - can we doubt that God's mercy extends to them?'* [7]

But, to return to Anderson, our conclusion with regard to his optimism is that it is not well founded in biblical terms and the fact that Packer and Stott, whose views we are about to consider, do not endorse it confirms that evaluation. But our feeling is that it was he who, more than anybody, secured a place for the salvation of the untold on the evangelical agenda.

BEING STRICTLY NEUTRAL

Under this heading we consider the views of J.I.Packer, expressed in an address which he gave at a consultation sponsored by the National Association of Evangelicals and Trinity Evangelical Divinity School in the United States in 1989. In his submission which was entitled 'Evangelicals and the Way Of Salvation', he identified four 'strong tendencies' which were at work in opposition to historic evangelical views on the doctrine of salvation. Two of these, the third and the fourth, related to faith and justification. The other two connect with our theme. They were:

> *'1 The question of salvation is less urgent than evan-gelicals have thought. This contention raises the issue of*

universalism, and the destiny of those who never heard the gospel'.

'2 The question of salvation is less agonizing than evangelicals have thought. This contention raises the issue of conditional immortality and the annihilation of unbelievers following the last judgment'.

Of all the theses which he presented, he regarded the first of these as 'the big one'. After a thorough critique of Universalism and an outline of the aspect of mystery in the basic elements of God's saving grace, Packer concluded;

'that all who are saved are saved by grace through faith, while all who perish do so through the fault of their own choice and impenitence'.[8]

He then took up the particular question of those who have not heard the gospel and their salvation, introducing it by an oft-quoted passage from Anderson, who had asked:

'Might it not be true of the follower of some other religion that the God of all mercy had worked in his heart by his Spirit, bringing him in some measure to realize his sin and need for forgiveness, and enabling him, in his twilight, as it were, to throw himself on God's mercy?'

To that Packer replied:

'The answer surely is; yes, it might be true, as it seems to have been true for some non-Israelites in Old Testament times: think of Melchizedek, Job, Naaman, Cyrus, Nebuchadnezzar, the sailors in Jonah's boat and the Ninevites to whom he preached, for starters.'

He continued however to say that:

'In heaven any such penitents will learn that they were saved by Christ's death and their hearts were renewed by

*the Holy Spirit and they will worship God accordingly.
Christians since the second century have voiced the hope
that there are such people, and we may properly voice the
same hope today'.[9]*

In the previous chapters we commented on the examples which
Packer lists and others too, claiming that they cannot be fairly used in
the argument because they had received some special revelation. We do
not therefore think that there is any need to answer Anderson's hypo-
thetically expressed question in the affirmative. To do so is an unnecessary concession, as is the view that general revelation even 'hints' at
mercy. Mercy is more than benevolence and beneficence combined; it
shows pity to the undeserving. Scripture Passages which speak of what
God reveals of himself apart from the gospel, for example Romans 1:
18-20 and Acts 14: 15-17, do not include that dimension at all. God is
wonderfully kind to sinners but his providences do not always appear
to be good. Some not only appear to be the reverse, but they could be
regarded as disclosing a merciless tyrant.

But we must note that Packer is only reckoning with a possibility
here, regarding it as conceivable that God might save some of the
unevangelised. This is to say that were he actually to do so, he would
not be 'denying himself', that is acting in a way which is contradictory
of his nature. But he goes on to affirm adamantly:

*'But - and this is the point to consider - we have no
warrant from Scripture to expect that God will act thus in
any single case where the Gospel is not yet known'.[10]*

This is why he comes into the category of being neutral on this matter.
It is interesting that Packer wants to remain firmly neutral on this
point, rather than becoming optimistic, for he is well aware that the
Westminster Confession of Faith offers a basis for optimism on this
point and within a Calvinistic framework. His non-endorsement of that
position, which is not the same as the case which Pinnock, Cotterell or
Anderson advance, and which we will refer to later, is therefore
significant. Quite categorically, he relates his neutrality on this matter

to the absence of undergirding scriptural testimony with regard to it. But it may be that he also feels that when anyone entertains any optimism on this point, it will inevitably have the effect of diminishing the urgency of the evangelistic and missionary task. Our reason for entertaining such a thought arises from the statement with which he concluded his submission. It is as follows:

> 'To cherish this hope therefore is not to diminish in the slightest our urgent and never-ending missionary obligation, any more than it is to embrace universalism as a basis for personal and communal living. Living by the Bible means assuming that no one will be saved apart from faith in Christ and acting accordingly'. [11]

That is practical exclusivism.

BEING MILDLY OPTIMISTIC

We turn to John Stott as an example of this viewpoint even though, distancing himself with respect from Anderson, he describes himself as 'agnostic' . He writes:

> 'Speaking now for myself, although I am attracted by Sir Norman Anderson's concept, and although there may be truth in it...I believe the most Christian stance is to remain agnostic on this question'. [12]

Given these words it may be wondered why we do not classify him alongside Packer. After all not much daylight can be seen between being neutral and being agnostic. We choose to keep them apart because while Packer professes no hope for the salvation of the unevangelised, Stott writes: 'However, ... I am imbued with hope' and he proceeds to give reasons for that. What are they?

We have quoted several comments on Acts 4:12 and on John 14:6 which, understandably, are often considered together when this subject is discussed. Stott's comment on these verses is clear and categorical. He does not use any evasive argument but upholds what he calls 'the plain, natural and obvious meaning' of John 14:6 and Acts 4:12 declaring:

> 'If there is only one Saviour, there can be only one way of
> salvation'.[13]

He regards this way of salvation as being inseparably bound up with three truths which he describes as 'the three truths which Evangelicals are at all costs determined to safeguard'. They are:

> 'that human beings left to themselves are perishing, and
> that they cannot save themselves, and that Jesus is the only
> qualified Saviour'.[14]

But he is prepared to entertain some questions because, in his view, they do not run cross-counter to those truths acknowledged. Those questions are:

> 'What condition has to be fulfilled in order that they may
> be saved? How much knowledge of Jesus do people have
> to have before they can believe in him? And how much
> faith do they have to exercise? Those who genuinely hear
> the gospel must repent and believe, of course. But what
> about those who have not heard it? They cannot save
> themselves, as we have seen, and Christ is the only
> Saviour. Is there then any way in which God will have
> mercy on them, through Christ alone, and not through
> their own merit?'[15]

Stott lists a number of options by way of answer to these questions which do not meet with his approval. Two of these are found in the inclusivist position of Vatican II (see chapter 2), which argues that those who seek God and strive to do good can be received by him, and derives a similar emphasis on good works from the parable of the sheep and the goats in Matthew 25. Next he also dismisses the notions that God knows how people would have responded if they had heard the gospel and that God gives a vision of Jesus to the dying in the last moments of their life. He then describes the view that there will be a preaching of the gospel in the next life as nothing but a guess, interpreting the 1 Peter verses as we have done and contra Pinnock. Finally, he sets aside Anderson's suggestion which we have considered. So, what is he left with?

His answer is not in terms of the seventeenth century confessions. It is made up of three strands. The first element in it is what Anderson argued about the heathen being in the same position as Old Testament people. He writes:

> 'What we do not know, however, is exactly how much knowledge and understanding of the gospel people need before they can cry to God for mercy and be saved. In the Old Testament, people were certainly "justified by grace through faith" even though they had little knowledge or expectation of Christ. Perhaps there are others today in a somewhat similar position. They know they are sinful before God, and that they cannot do anything to win his favour, so in self-despair they call upon the God they dimly perceive to save them. If God does save such, as many evangelical Christians tentatively believe, their salvation is still only by grace, only through Christ, only by faith'.[16]

We have already dealt with this argument but take the opportunity of repeating that we do not hold that no one could be saved before the coming of Christ or from outside the community of Israel. All we maintain is that they had some knowledge that God had promised a redeemer and not only that there was one God or that he was the God of Israel. That is something which Packer seems to overlook and Stott sets aside by saying 'they had little knowledge or expectation of Christ'. The fact is that they had enough to enable them not only to know their need and cry to God, but also to depend on a promised Saviour, though how much they knew of him is neither vital to the exclusivist case nor possible for us to state.

The second reason which Stott presents is that the Bible does not declare how God will deal with those who have never heard the gospel. That argument will be the main focus of the next chapter. We have already come across it in what Phillips has written.

The third reason is that he is sure that the Bible encourages him to be hopeful that more will be saved than will perish. In this connection he refers to the fact that God promised a countless posterity to Abraham and the book of Revelation records the fulfilment of that by mentioning that 'a great multitude that no-one could count, from every nation, tribe, people, language' stood before the throne of God and the Lamb. He also refers to Romans 5 where Paul teaches that the grace of God in the righteousness of Christ will gain a total triumph over sin and its consequences, introduced into the world by Adam.

Packer concluded his discussion of this matter with a reference to the missionary task of the church and its urgency, and so does Stott. But there is a most important difference to be observed between them which highlights the advantage of neutrality over optimism from a biblical point of view. Though Packer does not refer to Romans 10 when arguing that the Bible does not give any support for expecting salvation without faith (later he refers to it when he discusses faith), his neutrality does not *contradict* the teaching there. But Stott does refer to it in his closing remarks and has to alter the text so that his optimism can be maintained. He writes:

> 'It is hard for people to call on one they have not believed in, or to believe in one of whom they have not heard, or to hear if no-one preaches to them. It is easier for people to believe once they have heard the good news of Christ crucified'.[17]

But was Paul implying that it is hard? Surely, he was declaring that it was impossible.

THE ISSUE OF 'THE LAST BATTLE'

The 'non-theological' piece of literature to which we referred earlier is from the writings of C.S.Lewis. In the final volume of the Narnia series, *The Last Battle*, there is a discussion between a pagan named Emeth (which happens to be the Hebrew word for 'truth') and Lord Aslan.

Lewis writes from the standpoint of Emeth:

*'Then I fell at his feet, and thought, Surely this is the hour
of death, for the Lion (who is worthy of all honour) will
know that I have served Tash all my days and not him.
Nevertheless, it is better to see the Lion and die than to be
Tisroc of the world and live and not to have seen him. But
the Glorious One bent down his golden head and touched
my forehead with his tongue and said, Son, thou art
welcome. But I said, Alas, Lord I am no son of Thine but
the servant of Tash. He answered, Child, all the service
thou hast done to Tash, I account as service done to me.
then by reason of my great desire for wisdom and understanding, I overcame my fear and questioned the Glorious
One and said, Lord, is it then true as the Ape said, that
thou and Tash are one? The Lion growled so that the earth
shook (but his wrath was not against me) and said, It is
false. Not because he and I are one, but because we are
opposites, I take to me the services which thou hast done
to him. For I and he are of such different kinds that no
service which is vile can be done to me, and none which is
not vile can be done to him. Therefore, if any man swear
by Tash and keep his oath for oath's sake, it is by me that
he has truly sworn, though he know it not, and it is I who
reward him. And if any man do cruelty in my name, then,
though he says the name Aslan, it is Tash whom he serves
and by Tash his deed is accepted. Dost thou understand,
Child? I said Lord, thou knowest how much I understand.
But I said also (for the truth constrained me), Yet I have
been seeking Tash all my days. Beloved, said the Glorious
One, unless thy desire had been for me thou wouldst not
have sought so long and so truly. For all find what they
truly seek'.*[18]

It is not possible to measure what effect this statement has had among
evangelicals. This is not only because of the popularity of C.S.Lewis

and his writings, greater in the States than in the United Kingdom, but because people are so governed by subjectivism. A passage such as we have quoted can be admired from a literary point of view without its poisonous content being recognised. How many parents have read this to their children and, not noticing what it is saying have not corrected it? We hazard the guess that its influence has been far greater among unthinking evangelicals than that of the theologians.

THE SEVENTEENTH CENTURY CONFESSIONS

Even though exclusivism has been the unvarying position of the church throughout its history, it has not been the case that it has denied that certain categories of people, whose number cannot be specified, will be in heaven. These are children dying in infancy and those who are incapable of making a rational response to the gospel.

The evidence for this is found in the confessional statements which were drawn up in England in the seventeenth century. The Westminster Confession of 1643, the Savoy Declaration of 1658 and the 1689 Baptist Confession all refer to this matter and in almost identical terms. Taking the Westminster Confession declaration, as it was the first to be promulgated, we have the following statement in the chapter on 'Effectual Calling':

> 'Elect infants, dying in infancy, are regenerated and saved by Christ through the Spirit, who worketh when, and where, and how he pleaseth. So also are all other elect persons, who are incapable of being outwardly called by the ministry of the Word'.[19]

Although the Savoy Declaration leaves out the word 'elect' and the 1689 Confession omits the reference to 'the Spirit', there was quite clearly a consensus on this point among Presbyterians, Independents (Congregationalists) and Baptists. Two things however need to be said about this kind of 'optimism', if we may call it that.

The first is that it is grounded on a very different basis from the optimism which we have seen in Pinnock and Cotterell's writings. In these official documents, the inclusion of infants and the mentally handicapped in the scope of salvation is grounded on the work of the Holy Spirit immediately on the soul which reveals the Lord Jesus Christ as Saviour, in accord with the secret electing purpose of God. This ground is in keeping with the way the gospel works. It goes beyond the other kind of work which has been referred to - a preparatory one which causes concern, creates a sense of need and makes a person look Godwards. This work *bestows* salvation. It reveals Christ. It is like 'being born out of due time', not living 'in the twilight'.

Secondly, there are other statements in what these documents have to say about Effectual Calling which need to be taken into account. If the one just quoted opens a door, the one about to be quoted prevents it being swung open wider.

> *'Much less can men not professing the Christian religion be saved in any other way whatsoever, be they ever so diligent to frame their lives according to the light of nature and the law of that religion they do profess; and to assert that they may, is very pernicious, and to be detested.'*[20]

The conclusion to be drawn from these excepting clauses is that while there were ecclesiological and eschatological differences between those who drew them up, they were not incompatible with a gospel exclusivism. What is being presented today about the salvation of the unevangelised is out of keeping with the gospel though it speaks of faith in God, his grace and the blood of Christ.

But one further matter must be mentioned. It relates to a whole chapter which is only found in the Savoy Declaration. The Savoy Declaration and the 1689 Baptist Confession were modelled on the Westminster Confession and they only departed from it where it was judged necessary. Those departures were related either to points on which there was disagreement, for example with regard to the government of the church and to baptism, or else to a concern to make something quite clear which was believed to be important.

What we want to refer to is a chapter which is only found in the Savoy Declaration. It is called 'Of the Gospel, and of the Extent of the Grace thereof'. The Preface to the whole Declaration says with regard to its subject matter that it is:

'a Title that may well not be omitted in a Confession of Faith: In which Chapter, what is dispersed, and by intimation in the Assemblies' Confession, with some little addition, is here brought together, and more fully, under one head'.[21]

The chapter has four paragraphs. The first declares that the promise of the seed of the woman was the proclamation of the substance of the gospel, effective for the conversion of sinners. The fourth paragraph says that such a conversion is only the result of a sovereign work of the Holy Spirit. It is the second and third paragraphs which are materially relevant to our inquiry.

The third paragraph declares that to hear the gospel preached is a sovereign favour of God, graciously granted or withheld, and it is not part of intellectual improvement or 'common light'. The second paragraph is what we want to highlight. We therefore quote it in full. It reads:

'This promise of Christ, and salvation by him, is revealed only in and by the word of God; neither do the works of creation and providence, with the light of nature, make discovery of Christ, or of grace by him, so much as in a general or obscure way; much less that men, destitute of the revelation of him by the promise or gospel, should be enabled thereby to attain saving faith or repentance.'[22]

This declaration represents the substantial agreement among the churches in the post-Reformation era on this matter. It is that agreement which needs to be expressed today. It is in keeping with strong and compassionate missionary activity and, what is more important, with certain fixed points of Christian truth. We set these out in the next and final chapter.

Endnotes

1. Phillips op.cit. p.231

2. Christianity and World religions: The challenge of Pluralism IVP 1984 p.154

3. ibid.p.143

4. ibid.p.144

5. ibid p.146

6. ibid.pp.148,9

7. The Salvation of the Gentiles in Evangelical Review of Theology Vol 15 No 1 January 1991 pp.36-43

8. Evangelical Affirmations eds. Kenneth S. Kantzer & Carl F.H.Henry Zondervan 1990 pp.107ff.

9. ibid.p.123

10. ibid. p.123

11. ibid.p.123

12. Stott op.cit. p.327

13. ibid.p.324

14. ibid.p.324

15. ibid.p.324

16. The Contemporary Christian IVP 1992 pp.318,9

17. ibid. pp.319,20

18. The Last Battle Penguin London 1956 p.149

19. Confession of Faith and Subordinate Standards. Free Church of Scotland 1973 p.18

20. ibid.p.18

21. Schaff. The Creeds of Christendom. Vol 111 Baker 1983 p.715

22. The Savoy Declaration of Faith and Order. Evangelical Press 1971 p.30

Finding our bearings

O ur approach so far has been largely negative. That has been unavoidable. We have allowed those who believe that some who have not heard the gospel will nevertheless be saved, to present their arguments, and we have attempted to answer their arguments step by step. The main lines of the case which they present have now been covered and we hope that our answers have been convincing.

In this final chapter, we change tack. We will set out the case for the kind of exclusivism which we are persuaded is expressed in the Bible and which is reflected in the great evangelical confessions of the seventeenth century. We will do this by presenting some fixed points of biblical teaching which together form the framework within which this question must be settled, if it is to be settled in a way that is truly evangelical. We will assert that the Bible does have something to say and then present what we think that is.

THE BIBLE HAS SOMETHING TO SAY

We begin with this for two reasons. First, because the only basis on which any statement can claim even to be considered is that it has a foundation in Scripture. What the Bible says on any subject is, however, an important question only for those who make an evangelical profession. Those who do not do so, like the inclusivists and pluralists to whom we have referred, can plough their own furrow without feeling that they ought to bring their views to the bar of God's word. Evangelicals, however, cannot act like that and still expect to retain the name of evangelical without being challenged.

But secondly, we make this claim because the evangelical optimists whose views we have examined all declare that the Bible is either silent or unclear with regard to the destiny of the unevangelised. Though this is not as serious as an explicit setting aside of the Bible, it may be no less dangerous. While recognising that it does not tell us everything about God's purposes, we do need to be absolutely sure that we are not over-looking anything that Scripture does teach. We must neither ignore what Scripture says, nor claim a freedom to explore further than God's word has declared. To do either leaves the genuineness of our evangelical commitment open to question. The effect is bound to be detrimental or even disastrous, depending on the degree of importance of the subject under examination. The teaching of the Bible can be missed as well as dismissed.

The eternal destiny of the unevangelised is a matter of no slight concern. It has important associations with other doctrines and duties. Whatever may be argued to the contrary, it is intimately bound up with other gospel truths and practical duties like evangelistic preaching and missionary activity. It cannot be omitted without consequence. We therefore think it important to examine the claim that Scripture is silent on this subject to see if it is really so. Nothing should be assumed.

ARGUMENTS FOR SCRIPTURE'S SILENCE

In the debate at the annual conference of the Evangelical Missionary Alliance in 1989 Peter Cotterell argued that, as the fate of the unevangelised is not formally addressed in Scripture and is not decided there, it should be an open question in the church today. We find ourselves in strong disagreement not only with the conclusion presented but with the basic principle of such thinking.

Cotterell's way of thinking about Scripture gives too much importance to what its human authors intended to say in reply to the situations which they addressed and not enough to its divine authorship. It seems from what he said that he must limit what is authoritative in Scripture to what is directly related to the problems of those specifically addressed. But though the scriptures do have time-space contexts, they must, as God's word written for the church of all time, surely have a wider authority and relevance than to the restricted situations originally addressed.

A similar outlook is presented by Gary Phillips who argues that some degree of agnosticism on this matter is unavoidable, whatever one's final conclusion on the question might be. The reason which he gives for that is:

> 'At present, we must be partially agnostic; whether we like it or not, Scripture does not clearly make us privy to God's arrangements for the Untold. Apparently he did not feel it necessary to inform those to whom (by definition) those plans would never have immediate relevance'.[1]

Does not the destiny of the unevangelised 'have immediate relevance' for every church until the Lord returns? Has he not commanded it to take the gospel to the world? May we therefore not expect Scripture to address this subject?

But on the particular matter of the subject not being formally addressed as a church issue, we readily admit that the New Testament does not treat it in that way. An example of the kind of thing Cotterell is thinking of here would be the way in which, in his letter to churches in Galatia, Paul deals with the covenantal status of Gentiles who believe in Jesus. The question of the salvation of the unevangelised is not highlighted in that way. Does this mean that the Bible has *nothing whatsoever* to say about it? No. All it shows is that it was not a matter which was agitating the churches of the first century and that, consequently, the apostles did not need to deal with it at length.

The apparent omission of a formal treatment is, however, a double-edged sword in relation to our present argument. Instead of providing a loophole for the case for optimism, it can be appealed to by exclusivists in support of their own case. They would point out that there was no uncertainty among the churches of the apostolic era about the destiny of those who did not hear the gospel.

Both Sir Norman Anderson and John Stott give evidence in their writings of similar thinking regarding Scripture's silence. Anderson actually writes that:

> 'Many Protestant theologians, indeed, believe that we must leave at this point the question of the eternal destiny

*of all those who have never heard the gospel, since the
Bible does not seem to provide any explicit solution to this
problem'.*[2]

By contrast with these he chooses to explore the subject positively
because he believes that it is an area which is biblically undefined.

Stott also makes use of the argument of Scripture's silence or lack of
clarity when facing up to this question. He writes:

> *'We need to combine confidence and agnosticism, what
> we know (because Scripture plainly teaches it) and what
> we do not know (because Scripture is either unclear or
> even silent about it)'.*[3]

As an example of what we know from Scripture and can be confident
about, Stott cites the fact that it clearly denies any possibility of self-
salvation. But what happens to the unevangelised after death is an
example of what we cannot know and must be agnostic about. This is,
he says, because Scripture does not record:

> *'exactly how much knowledge and understanding of the
> gospel people need before they can cry to God for mercy
> and be saved'.*[4]

While we grant that such information is not given in the Bible, we
would question whether this proves that Scripture is unclear about
whether the unevangelised can be saved. Here is a place where a parallel
can be drawn between the evangelised and the unevangelised. It can be
done like this. Scripture does not give exact detail of how much anyone
who hears the gospel *must know* in order to be saved? Does that lead us
to say that Scripture is unclear about the way of salvation? It is one
thing to say what must be made known to them. Scripture is clear about
that. But it is another thing to decide how much of that they *must
understand*, and Scripture is not clear about that. The same applies to
the unevangelised. What they do not or cannot know about the gospel
must not be allowed to determine whether Scripture is unclear about
their condition and need.

Stott then uses the limited knowledge of Old Testament saints to buttress his case for the unevangelised being saved, because he declares that neither group could be said to have full knowledge of the way of salvation. But, as has been pointed out a number of times, however small the knowledge which Old Testament saints had, small that is in relation to the fulfilment, they did have the promise which, by definition, those who are unevangelised have never been informed about. Their cases therefore are not analogous and so the argument based on a link between them proves neither the possibility of the salvation of the unevangelised, nor the silence of Scripture on this issue.

ARGUMENT AGAINST SCRIPTURE'S SILENCE

We believe that Scripture does have something to say about the destiny of the unevangelised. Indeed, no one should be surprised at that. If we reflect a little more on the claim that Scripture is silent or unclear on this matter, regarding it as being even possibly the case, we have to face a very strange situation. Given that the primary focus, and main story line, of the Bible in all its sixty-six books is the salvation of mankind by the gospel, the destiny of the unevangelised is not a million miles away from this theme. The condition of mankind apart from that salvation is but the other side of this redemptive coin. To declare that the Bible which speaks with such a wealth of detail and at such length about salvation, has nothing whatsoever to say about their destiny, apart from that gospel, is a tall order. Is it not much more likely, to put it no higher, that the condition of people without that gospel would be presented in the book which speaks about their salvation? If the Bible presents salvation as a necessity and not an option, which it does, should we not expect it to say why that is so and from what people need to be saved? What the Bible says on those matters is also relevant to the question with which we are concerned in this book. The destiny of the unevangelised and the necessity of salvation are twin themes.

WHAT THEN DOES THE BIBLE HAVE TO SAY?

As the gospel of God's grace is presented in various ways throughout the Bible, so is the condition of human beings apart from it. There is however, one part of Scripture which we think is particularly relevant to this subject - the Epistle to the Romans. For Romans focuses explicitly on two matters: the gospel itself and its universal relevance. Cotterell is correct to speak of:

> *'the teaching of Paul in his systematic exposition of his gospel in Romans'.*[5]

The only clue which the apostle gives as to his purpose in writing the letter is couched in terms which are too general for any exact identification to be made. (15:15) But whatever his precise aim or aims might have been, it is clear from the letter itself that two factors had entered into his reckoning and that he understood that an exposition of the gospel would be relevant to them.

The first was that he was hoping to take the gospel to Spain, and Rome would have been a most convenient stopping place en route. He had neither founded the church there nor been able to visit it, though he had often hoped to do so. To present his gospel would have been a good way of preparing for such a visit and gaining support for his journey to Spain (Romans 1: 8-13;15: 20-32).

Secondly, he had heard that there were some difficulties between Jewish and Gentile believers in the church which threatened its unity (14;1-15:7), and a statement of the gospel would remind them of their oneness and their duty to receive each other notwithstanding their differences.

Even so, it is quite clear that Paul's desire to preach the gospel in Rome was related to the fact that it was the capital of 'the world' at that time (Romans 1:14-16). Jews were to be found there and so were Gentiles - whether educated according to the standards of the day or not - that is Greeks and barbarians. His readiness to preach the gospel to all was related both to his confidence that it was God's power to save and to his realisation that it was needed by people of all races. The gospel of Christ is for the world; the world of mankind needs it. Without it, mankind presents a sordid and hopeless picture.

Pinnock raises the following question :

'Why in Acts does Paul sound more generous than he does in Romans?'

By the reference to Acts he has in mind what Paul said to the people of Lystra and to the meeting of the Areopagus in Athens (Acts 14:16,17 & 17: 22-31). He understands the first of these as signifying that

'God had a gracious understanding of their past and of their culture'.

The second he comments on as follows:

'Evidently Paul thought of these people as believers in a certain sense, in a way that could be and should be fulfilled in Jesus Christ.'[6]

Taking such a view of these passages in Acts, it is not surprising that Pinnock raises his question about Romans. He does not solve his problem by saying, as others do, that there is a real contradiction between Acts and Romans. What he says is that exclusivist interpreters have not understood Paul correctly, either in Acts or in Romans. After putting his question he comments by way of reply:

'The assumption is that we are right in reading Romans in a pessimistic manner. It may be that Romans is more generous than we have assumed'.[7]

Pinnock's conclusion about what Romans has to say is:

'(Paul) is insisting that humanity cannot save itself apart from the work of God in redemption. But it is wrong to read into his words in Romans the idea that he is denying that many Jews and Gentiles in the past have responded positively to God on the basis of this light, as Luke also intimates in the book of Acts'.[8]

We proceed to examine the opening chapters of Romans and do so by making use of Paul's expression 'There is no difference'. This will enable us to set out the case for exclusivism as well as to answer Pinnock.

'THERE IS NO DIFFERENCE'

Paul uses this expression twice in his exposition of the gospel. He brackets Jews and Gentiles by saying that there is no difference between them in certain respects. He includes people from all nations, intending to bring everyone within the scope of the major statements which he makes. Whatever distinctions exist or may be thought to exist between human beings, they do not apply at those points where the word of God through the apostle binds them all together.

What are those points of non-difference? Paul uses this common denominator to refer first to human sin and then to divine grace. The fact of sin and the fact of grace are the focal points of the gospel. 'All have sinned' announces the first of these facts (Rom. 3:23); 'the same Lord is Lord of all and richly blesses all who call upon him' (10:12) declares the second. There are no distinctions to be made between human beings with regard to those facts. Sin is common to all for reasons which are given, and grace is available to all on the terms laid down. These emphases make the case for exclusivism, outlawing any optimism which wants to create a difference where the Bible will not allow one to be made.

NO DIFFERENCE IN RELATION TO SIN

Paul argues that both Jew and Greek are 'under sin' (3:9) and then proceeds to quote from several Old Testament passages to prove it. Using the Old Testament as he does is in itself significant, because it means taking what was originally addressed to the Israelites and extending its truth to Gentiles as well. Evidently, Paul did not think that it was necessary for someone to know Scripture before he could sin and be held guilty for it. The charge that no one seeks God and no one fears

God is therefore not only applicable to the Jew who had the Scriptures, but to the Gentile as well. Sin characterises every human being because of his relationship to Adam (5:12)

Of course, Paul is neither overlooking nor denying the reality of special revelation which the Jew had and which the Gentile did not. He specifically refers to that distinction in 2: 14,15 and 3: 1, 2. But though the Jew had the distinct advantage of having received the oracles of God, prophecies of redemption as well as precepts relating to conduct, this did not actually result in their being nearer to God than the Gentiles who were not favoured with such disclosures. Though privileged, they were no better than the Gentiles. All were under sin (3:9) and accountable to God.

But Paul also says that all were 'under law' (3:19). How could this be if Gentiles did not have the oracles of God? His answer is that they were not without all revelation of God. This came to them in a different way from that which God used to reveal himself to his ancient people. It was not via laws in a book, the Ten Commandments given at Sinai. It was by the unveiling of God's transcendence that is his eternal power and wisdom in the created universe (1:19,20), and the recording of his moral requirements in their constitution as human beings (2:14). The Gentile was made in the image and likeness of God not one whit less than the Jew. Their environment spoke to them of God and so did their very nature. In that sense they knew God (1:21): they had some awareness of his majesty as he had revealed himself in the works of his hands, and of his morality by means of the sense of right and wrong they possessed. They knew that they were accountable to him as their judge (1:19, 20 & 32; and 2:14,15). But there is no hint in Scripture that such self-disclosure on the part of God contains any intimation of his being merciful to sinners; kind and good, yes but merciful, no.

It is an essential part of the case for exclusivism to assert, and to do justice to, the fact that everyone has received some light about God and from God. No one is left in total ignorance that there is a God and that he is to be worshipped and served. However, what must be closely combined with this is the fact of human rebellion against this God; everyone's rebellion. The Gentile tries to put out the light which he has been given by excluding God from his thinking about the world and himself, creating his own world view (1:21, 28). This is because he is born a sinner and as such, loves darkness (1:32).

Though he has only limited revelation to go by, the Gentile has an inveterate desire to oppose it in its mental and moral significance. His manufacture of idols and fabrication of ideas are proof of how perverse he is (1:21-25). False religion is not an attempt to find what is true but a flight from God and from reason. For a Gentile, who has not read Scripture or heard anything from it to be condemned, is therefore not unjust. What would be unjust would be if he were to be punished as the Jew who was given more light. What Paul says about the Gentile is what applies to those who have never heard the gospel.

The Jew has the oracles of God, but he too is a sinner. It is not only the Gentile who has fallen: Adam was the father and head of all mankind. The same inner propensity to evil which operates in the Gentile inclines the Jew to refuse to face the extra revelation which he has been given. Instead he twists it; applying prohibitions to others, he contents himself with not infringing them outwardly (2:1-3;17-24). He trusts in himself rather than in the grace of God, blind to the Messiah who is promised in the sacred oracles with which he has been entrusted (10:2-4).

The net effect of all this is that all human beings are guilty before God. Because they have light, whether much or little, and because they refuse to live in accord with it, they are without excuse. The same unbelief which disposes the Gentile to reject the light he has, would lead him to reject also the light which the Jew was given, had he been given that as well. On the day of judgment no one, neither Gentile nor Jew, will have any defence to present against God's justice and they will know it is so. 'Every mouth will be silenced and all the world held accountable to God' (3:19). There is no possibility of a good pagan because 'there is no one who does good, not even one' (3:12) and that applies to devotees of every religion.

NO DIFFERENCE IN REGARD TO GRACE

What we have said so far is a direct refutation of how pluralists and inclusivists regard the condition of human beings before God. But though evangelical optimists do not deny the fact of universal human sinfulness, they may underestimate its gravity. The truth is that no one can be saved in whom the reign of sin has not been broken. God must intervene to accomplish that or everyone remains 'dead in . . . transgressions and sins...by nature objects of wrath' (Ephesians 2:1,3). The Lord Jesus said 'I tell you the truth, no-one can enter the kingdom of God unless he is born of water and of the Spirit. Flesh gives birth to flesh but the Spirit gives birth to spirit' (John 3:5,6). Without that mysterious activity no one would believe, however many times he might hear the gospel.

By placing such emphasis on the sovereign activity of the Holy Spirit, we are not claiming that absolutely nothing can happen in the human heart until the gospel is preached. We glory in the reverse being true. The Spirit is a Person; the word is only an instrument or means. The Spirit of God can and does work immediately upon the soul, without means. Consequently, neither the spiritual deadness of the unbeliever, nor the disobedient failure of a believer to communicate the gospel, presents an insuperable obstacle for God - 'the God who gives life to the dead and calls things that are not as though they were' (Romans 4:17). It is on this basis that the seventeenth century confessions spoke of the salvation of infants and the mentally handicapped, those incapable of reasoning and of speech. God would apply gospel grace to them directly via regeneration.

But what is at issue between exclusivists and evangelical optimists is what applies to those who are capable of understanding the gospel but have never heard it. Here we come to Romans 10 which contains the second use of the expression 'There is no difference'. This use refers to the method of grace in the era in which God has revealed his saving righteousness via the incarnation and atonement of the eternal Son of God. This gracious activity 'justifies the wicked' (Romans 4:5) but it requires faith in Christ, in his death and in him as Lord. (1:16; 3:21,22; 24-26; 27-31; 4: 22-25; 5:1; and 10: 8-13). Such faith is required of Jew and Greek, that is of every single person.

Paul equates trusting in the Lord with calling on his name. Quoting from several passages in the Old Testament he makes it clear that what is being required in the gospel era is basically the same as what was called for in the past. That requirement was and is 'Everyone who calls on the name of the Lord will be saved'. There is but one way to salvation taught in both Testaments: it is calling on the name of the Lord. There never has been and there never will be any other. The name of the Lord simply means God revealed in the Saviour, the Lord Jesus Christ.

Paul immediately asks 'How then can they call on the one they have not believed in? And how can they believe in the one of whom they have not heard?' Those are the very questions of the evangelical optimists, though Paul voices them in a different tone and with a different aim. Here then is the point at which Paul could provide the optimists' answer that it is only necessary for people to believe in God not the Lord Jesus Christ, and to trust in God's mercy and not in Christ's death. That would settle the argument. But giving such an answer to the seemingly intractable situation which he has set up would mean his saying that there is a difference after all! He would be saying that those who hear of Christ have to believe in him, while those who have not do not have to - all they have to do is to turn to God. but that is not what Paul says. Rather he asserts, 'There is no difference...the same Lord is Lord of all and richly blesses all who call on him'. And that Lord is Jesus who died and rose again (10: 9). So all have to believe in Christ.

Well then, 'how can they believe in the one of whom they have not heard?' Paul's answer could not be clearer. They cannot; they have to hear. And to hear they have to be told. Preachers need to go and tell them and even they cannot go without being sent. It may seem that God is making salvation impossible or very difficult but the truth is that no one even deserves to hear the gospel, let alone be saved without it. Indeed, to hear the gospel is a demonstration of God's mercy. He is not putting obstacles in the way. He has brought the word down from heaven to earth and up from the grave in the Lord Jesus Christ. He has not acted in a corner (Acts 26:26). There is therefore an immense responsibility on Christian people, and especially on the ambassadors of Christ, to carry the gospel and to make the message clear and plain.

There are two questions relating to Paul's teaching in Romans which must be answered before we conclude our study. The first is connected with Romans 10 and the second with Romans 2.

Romans 10:12-18

The strong bearing of these verses on the subject of the destiny of the unevangelised should be obvious. Even Anderson writes that these verses form 'One of the most explicit passages in the New Testament on this subject'. But he side-steps their obvious meaning and force, claiming that Paul was not intending to exclude the possibility of those who had not heard the word coming to a knowledge of God. In support of this view, he quotes what Calvin says on Romans 10. Commenting on verses 14 and 15 he writes:

> '*But were any on this account to contend that God cannot transfer to men the knowledge of himself, except by the instrumentality of preaching, we deny that to teach this was the Apostle's intention; for he had only in view the ordinary dispensation of God, and did not intend to prescribe a law for the distribution of his grace*'.[9]

It is vital that we understand what Calvin is saying here, and what he is not saying. To do that we must look at other comments he makes on these verses about the knowledge which the unevangelised possess.

First of all we note that the opening words of the above quotation indicate that it is a part of an argument. Its context is therefore important. What Calvin says immediately before the part which Anderson quotes is:

> '*It belongs not indeed to us to imagine a God according to what we may fancy; we ought to possess a right knowledge of him, such as is set forth in his word. And when any one forms an idea of God as good, according to his own understanding, it is not a sure or a solid faith which he has, but an uncertain and evanescent imagination; it is therefore necessary to have the word, that we may have a right knowledge of God. No other word has he mentioned here but that which is preached, because it is the ordinary mode which the Lord has appointed for conveying his word*'.[10]

Clearly Calvin is making a distinction between two kinds of knowledge. There is the knowledge of God which comes by means of the word, and that he describes as 'right'. The other knowledge of God is described as 'imagination' and 'not a sure and solid faith'. Calvin is therefore not equating that kind of knowledge which someone who has never heard the gospel may possess, with the faith which is necessary for salvation. There is a real knowledge of God which is not saving. This is eloquently supported by what he says on Acts 10:4. He writes:

> 'Yet here a question may be asked, Whether faith require the knowledge of Christ, or it be content with the simple persuasion of the mercy of God? For Cornelius seemeth to have known nothing at all concerning Christ. But it may be proved by sound proofs that faith cannot be separated from Christ; for if we lay hold upon the bare majesty of God, we are rather confounded by his glory, than that we feel any taste of his goodness. Therefore, Christ must come between, that the mind of man may conceive that God is merciful. And it is not without cause that he is called the image of the invisible God, (Col.1.15;) because the Father offereth himself to be holden in his face alone. Moreover, seeing that he is the way, the truth, and the life, (John 14.6); whithersoever thou goest without him, thou shalt be enwrapped on every side in errors, and death shall meet you on every side'.[11]

The second thing to note is that the knowledge which the unevangelised possess is the kind of knowledge which is gained from God's created handiwork. Calvin writes on the use of Psalm 19 in Romans 10:

> 'God has already from the beginning manifested his divinity to the Gentiles, though not by the preaching of men, yet by the testimony of his creatures; for though the gospel was then silent among them, yet the whole workmanship of heaven and earth did speak and make known its author by its preaching. It hence appears, that the

*Lord, even during the time in which he confined the
favour of his covenant to Israel, did not yet so withdraw
from the Gentiles the knowledge of himself, but that he
ever kept alive some sparks of it among them. He indeed
manifested himself then more particularly to his chosen
people, so that the Jews might be justly compared to
domestic hearers, whom he familiarly taught as it were by
his own mouth; yet as he spoke to the Gentiles at a
distance by the voice of the heavens, he showed by this
prelude that he designed to make himself known at length
to them also.'*[12]

Calvin's emphasis, in the passage which Anderson quotes in support
of his case, is on the 'ordinary' way in which God saves, which is by
means of the preaching of the word. His recognition that God is able,
and may be pleased to bestow gospel grace without using any means
such as the preaching of the word, is but a recognition of God's sover-
eignty and not a claim that he actually does so. It is akin to what we
have noted from the seventeenth century confessions. Calvin is not
saying the same thing as the evangelical optimists. In fact he is arguing
for the inadequacy of any knowledge and faith which is not informed
by the word concerning Christ.

Romans 2: 5-16

Some may wonder how this passage fits in the exclusivist scheme or
indeed whether it can fit in at all. Judging from the way in which
Cotterell uses it, he is convinced that they cannot. He describes the
people to whom he thinks verses 14-16 apply as follows:

*'There are people who earnestly seek after God, seek to do
what is right, even acting contrary to the religion into
which they were born, so as to pursue the truth, although
the truth that is in Christ has never been preached to them.
Of such people Paul comments...'*[13]

The words which we have underlined above relate to the point which we wish to make. No one should think that the possibility which Cotterell outlines in his statement is being disputed. On the contrary, Cornelius and Lydia in Acts 10 and 16 were examples of this *at one time*. What is being challenged is that it was such people as Cotterell describes whom Paul had in mind when he wrote Romans 2:14-16.

The specification of 'Gentiles' in verse 14 refers to the 'Greek' in the immediately preceding verses. They are therefore the non-Jewish inhabitants of the world and not a sub-section of them which is what Cotterell's view requires. These Gentiles (literally 'nations') do not have the law of God as the Jews did. But Paul teaches that they were not wholly destitute of any knowledge of divine requirements because such were registered in their very constitution as human creatures. In addition, Paul makes clear that they were subject to the rebukes of their consciences and also liable to the judgment of God. They are therefore in the same boat as all the rest of mankind as far as sin, judgment and condemnation are concerned. Verses 6-11 have the potential of being much more serviceable to Cotterell's case but he does not use them. We therefore turn to those verses.

2:6-11

The whole context of this passage is about judgment. At the beginning of it Paul quotes from Psalm 62:12 saying that God 'will give to each person according to what he has done'. He concludes by declaring that 'God does not show favouritism'. Those statements by themselves assert the rectitude of God's justice to every individual, which is the foundation of the condemnation of all referred to in 3:19. That constitutes no problem for exclusivism.

But in between those two statements about God, the apostle divides human beings into two groups describing them according to their characteristics and conduct. He says of 'those who by persistence in doing good seek glory, honour and immortality' that they will be given 'eternal life', whether Jew or Gentile. The question is whether Paul is teaching salvation by works at this point and whether there is hope for the unevangelised on this basis.

It is always possible that some will argue that here we have salvation by works. But the cost of doing so is immense. They really have to conclude that Paul is hopelessly at odds with himself, teaching salvation by works on the one hand and by grace through faith on the other. This is because, quite explicitly, he defines faith as that which operates 'apart from works' in the matter of acceptance with God (4:4-6). This is too high a price to pay. Another explanation must be sought.

We must remember that Paul's aim in Romans 2 is to prove that Jews are as exposed to divine judgment as are the Gentiles, in spite of the fact that many advantages had been conferred upon them. They have turned their privileged position into a belief that they were favourites of God. Paul writes to demolish this and to show that mere possession of the law would not save them. Judgment is related to tenor of life and to conduct, not to outward privilege, just as it is not related to the lack of it. It is a life which seeks the glory and honour of God and immortality as a goal beyond the grave which will stand in the judgment, and that applies to everyone. This does not teach salvation by works; it teaches that works display character and that character is related to grace and to faith.

Our conclusion is therefore that neither Romans 2 nor Romans 10 contradict the exclusivist case. But each has something important to say to those who espouse it.

Romans 2 makes clear that all will stand in the judgment, and works will not be unimportant. The standard is just and righteous. Heaven is for the righteous and even those who seek for glory, honour and immortality (for life with God) are not worthy to enter it in and of themselves. A faith which does not result in such a life is not a faith at all. Not only will the unevangelised be judged, professing Christians will be judged too.

Romans 10 insists not only that faith must be 'in the heart' but that Jesus Christ, the one who died and rose again, must be trusted in. This is because his is the only perfect righteousness a sinner can have to enable him to stand before God in the judgment. All seeking after glory and honour and immortality is shot through with sin too, from God's point of view. It is not only the case that one's works cannot save; even one's faith cannot save. It is only Christ's righteousness that can save, and that is made freely available to any and to all on the basis of faith in him.

It is therefore essential to believe in him, but that is no immense task.The immense step has been taken, downward. The Son of God has become incarnate. He has lived and died and been raised again! The gospel has been made known. It involves no more, but no less, than the response of calling on him to become one's Saviour - 'And as the Scripture says "Anyone who trusts in him will never be put to shame"'.

CONCLUSION

We have argued that the Bible teaches that the unevangelised cannot be saved. As that sounds very negative we want to make three positive comments in conclusion.

The first is that God is a Saviour of sinners and he works sovereignly in saving them. He can save those who are constitutionally incapable of understanding the gospel, working directly and mysteriously in their hearts, evangelising them personally before they die. He can also save people when they are no longer being spoken to by others about the gospel. He can bring back to mind and conscience the instruction of parents and grandparents; Sunday school or Bible Class teachers, sermons from preachers and testimonies from friends in a split second and, in the words of the old memorable couplet;

'Between the stirrup and the ground
He mercy sought and mercy found'.

God's gracious work is not tied to the moments when the gospel is being preached. He is 'forgiving and good, abounding in love to all who call' on him (Psalm 86:5).

Secondly, while we have argued that the unevangelised cannot be saved, we would prefer to say that the unevangelised must be evangelised. This is no sleight of hand, an attempt to evade or ignore the awfulness of eternal and conscious separation from God's blessedness and unending subjection to his holy wrath of all sinners who do not believe the gospel. We believe that, but take no delight in it. We humble ourselves before the God who will exalt himself by judging sin, sinners and Satan, in a way which is most just. But we are living in the day of grace and the door to heaven is wide open to all who will come to God through Jesus Christ. The just God takes 'no pleasure in the death of the wicked but rather that they turn from their ways and live' (Ezekiel 33:11). We therefore prefer to put the matter this way round to remind ourselves that we are not to be satisfied with a defence of exclusivism, important though that is. Indeed, maintaining such a position, our responsibility is increased.

But finally, not only do the unevangelised need to be evangelised, the pluralists and inclusivists need to understand the gospel and the evangelical optimists need to become fully evangelical. The main focus of this book has been on the latter and their views. The position which they advocate has no exegetical basis in the Bible. It is special pleading. It is an academic luxury and it appears to be governed more by sentiment than by Scripture. It diminishes the grim seriousness of the universal human situation and the urgent necessity for the gospel to be made known.

Evangelical optimists claim that their position does not deny the importance and obligation of doing this. We question this on two levels, the level of teaching and practice.

First, on the level of teaching. Neither Cotterell nor Pinnock denies that the gospel is to be preached, but there are certain corollaries of what they teach which question the need of doing so. As Cotterell argues that some who have not heard the gospel will not be condemned, perhaps it would be better to keep all in ignorance of it. Telling them of the Lord Jesus Christ runs the risk that they will not believe in him and that as a result they will be exposed to judgment. Not telling them leaves the hope that they may be saved by means of the light they have. Salvation becomes more likely without the gospel than by means of it! This just cannot be true.

Pinnock argues that some will be saved without having heard the gospel while they were on earth and others will be saved by hearing the gospel after they have died. This makes the preaching of the gospel on earth non-essential. That cannot be true either.

Both views turn the Bible on its head and in particular the mandate of the Lord Jesus Christ to go into all the world with the gospel to every creature. As he was about to leave this earth and return to heaven, the Lord commanded his apostles, and through them his church, to ' go and make disciples of all nations, baptising them in the name of the Father and of the Son and of the Holy Spirit'. Did he send them on an unnecessary task, a fool's errand? Or is their going out into all the world with the gospel as essential in its own way, as was his coming down into it?

And on the level of practice, what will be the effect of such thinking on the churches? Or was it the condition of the churches which spawned the thinking in the first place? Here is the proverbial chicken and egg situation. Is it the church's attachment to academic respectability which has given rise to these views? It may be. But all the traffic is not one-way. Could it not be that the influence of materialism and secularism on Christian people has resulted in a concentration on the here and now and on the body, rather than on the eternal and on the soul? Whichever way, this easier doctrine has been developed and is being strongly argued at a time when the church is not at her best.

And what will its effect be? Will more people go to the mission field? What kind of people will go? Will they be like Judson, Carey, Paton, Moffatt, Martyn, Studd, Hudson Taylor? Will people at home support missions with giving and with prayer? Will they tell their relatives and neighbours about the Lord Jesus Christ? Evangelical optimists say their position is not detrimental to the spread of the gospel; but that claim has a hollow ring. The proof is otherwise.

The history of world mission bears forceful witness here. The era of missionary concern and expansion rose out of the Great Awakening associated with Whitefield and the Wesleys at the end of the eighteenth century. When that blessing shook down into the churches, Christians were shaken up and 'the world became their parish'. By contrast, the churches in the western world are in decline not only numerically and financially but morally, doctrinally and spiritually. Is this a time to argue for the salvation of the unevangelised? Is it not rather a time to assert the necessity of taking the gospel where 'Christ is not named'?

Endnotes

1. Phillips op.cit. p.243
2. Anderson op.cit.p.148
3. Stott The Contemporary Christian p.318
4. ibid. p.319
5. Cotterell op. cit. p.64
6. Pinnock op. cit. p.33
7. ibid. p.33
8. ibid. p.33
9. Calvin Commentary on Romans Eerdmans 1955 p.398
10. ibid. p.398
11. Calvin Commentary on Acts Vol 1 Eerdmans 1955 p.413
12. op.cit.Romans p.403
13. Cotterell op.cit.p.78

General Index

Index of Bible References

Index of Bible References